1001
unbelievable
FACTS

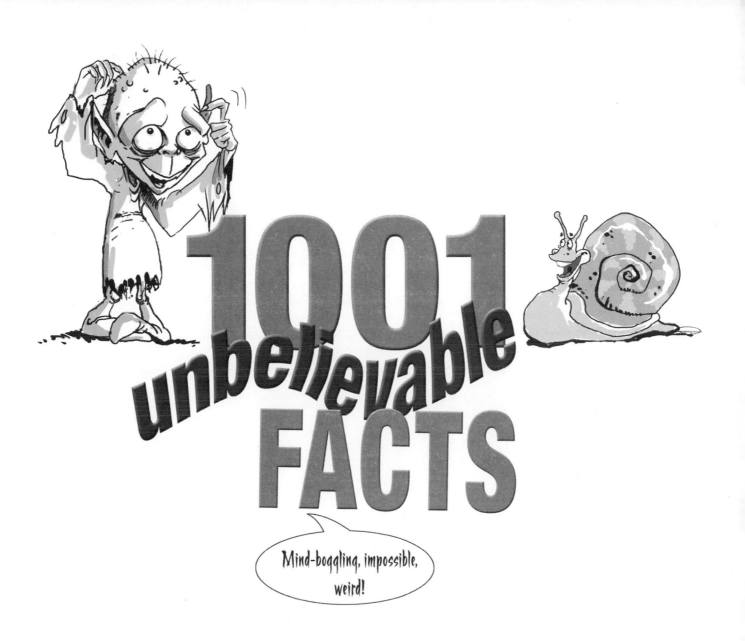

1001 unbelievable FACTS

Mind-boggling, impossible, weird!

Helen Otway

ARCTURUS

ARCTURUS

This edition published in 2015 by Arcturus Publishing Limited
26/27 Bickels Yard, 151–153 Bermondsey Street,
London SE1 3HA

Design & Illustration by quadrum▪

Goblin cover illustration by Steve Beaumont
Author: Helen Otway
Editors: Fiona Tulloch and Kate Overy

ISBN: 978-1-84193-783-0
CH000501US
Supplier 29, Date 0715, Print run 4362

Printed in China

CONTENTS

1001 Unbelievable Facts

Have you ever stopped to think about all the unbelievable things that are going on in the world? In the time it's taken you to read that sentence, hundreds of unimaginable things have just happened ... and that's hard to believe too!

Even before there were people on the planet to decide whether something was unbelievable or not, a whole range of unimaginable stuff was going on. *Tyrannosaurus rex*, for example, had incredible jaws full of foot-long teeth that were strong enough to crush a car! Then there was the gigantic *Brachiosaurus*—it was the length of two buses and weighed at least 77,161 pounds (35 metric tons)!

As soon as people came along, they would often spend their days looking for crazy things to do, ranging from making fire with a couple of sticks to building huge structures without any machinery whatsoever. Over time, scientists came out as the champions of inconceivable truths and often made unbelievable discoveries without even meaning to!

Rubber Duck Facts:

(Free extras, not part of your 1001 facts!)

You don't have to be a scientist to do something unbelievable, of course. Doing something simple like collecting rubber ducks is incredible too . . . if you have more than 2,580, like world record holder Charlotte Lee. Here are some other things you probably don't know about rubber ducks:

Queen Elizabeth II has a rubber duck that wears a crown! After this flabbergasting fact was revealed in the media in 2001, UK rubber duck sales increased by 80 percent.

In Dublin, Ireland, 150,000 rubber ducks took part in the largest-ever rubber duck race in 2006.

Thousands of rubber ducks were lost from a tanker during a Pacific storm in 1992 and were washing up all over the world for more than a decade afterward. Their movements have provided valuable information about ocean currents.

A rubber duck known as 'Duckie' has his very own website, which details his various vacations around the world. Fans can view photographs, read his blog updates and even respond to his appeal for a suitable female duck partner.

Get Going!

So, are you ready to read 1,001 astounding, amazing and totally unbelievable facts? Then let's get started...

Don't go there!

Run the 100 meters as many times as you like and see how your time compares to the world record. Study the nearest newborn baby and check if he or she really does blink only once or twice a minute (clapping to make a baby blink doesn't count). But please, please, please don't try any of the dangerous stuff mentioned in this book. Whenever you ride your bike, for example, keep your hands on the handlebar at all times and don't try to take it through any tunnels of fire, okay? Be sensible and you'll live to see another unbelievable day!

Unbelievable
Body Facts

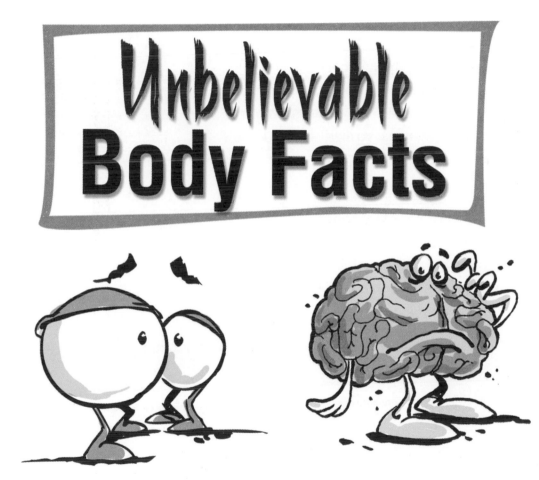

Whether your hair is curly or straight depends on the shape of your hair follicles: curly hair grows from oval follicles, straight hair grows from round follicles.

The average human body is made up of more than 50 trillion cells.

A Michigan couple opened a package delivered to their home and were shocked to find a liver and an ear inside! The parts should have been delivered to a nearby research laboratory.

Retrieving a memory takes 0.0004 second.

You have no control over some of your muscles! These are known as *involuntary muscles*, which the body uses for functions such as breathing and digesting food.

If you're right-handed, you tend to chew food on the right side of your mouth; if you're left-handed, you tend to chew on the left.

An operation on a patient in a Belgrade, Serbia, hospital was disrupted when two surgeons started a fight! They took their fistfight outside and the assistant surgeon completed the procedure.

Tooth enamel is the hardest substance in your body.

There are hundreds of viruses that can give you a cold. That's why there's no cure!

Hemochromatosis is a hereditary iron overload disorder—iron accumulates in the body, damaging the organs and darkening the skin.

Your brain is your hungriest organ!
Twenty percent of what you eat feeds it.

The painkilling drug aspirin comes from willow bark and was first described by Hippocrates in the 5th century BC.

A British retiree who lost her false teeth discovered that her dog had eaten them! The dog had a 3-hour operation to have them removed.

Red blood cells are made inside your bones. Each cell travels around the body about 250,000 times before it returns to the spleen to die.

Your eyes always close when you sneeze.

Your digestive system will process about 110, 231 pounds (50 metric tons) of food in your lifetime.

Sometimes a muscle fully contracts by itself when you're not expecting it and is very painful—that's a cramp!

Wreaths, pictures, jewelry, and postcards that are made of or contain human hair are on display in Leila's Hair Museum, in Missouri. These keepsakes were commonly made in Victorian times.

Florida girl Jennifer Mee hiccuped continuously for 5 weeks! The hiccups stopped as suddenly as they had started.

One person in 20 has an extra pair of ribs.

In an emergency, your body produces a hormone called *adrenaline* that gives you superhuman strength!

Pain signals reach the brain more slowly than touch signals. That's why rubbing things better really works!

There are more than 700 kinds of bacteria lurking in your large intestine.

Astronauts have to wear a *maximum absorption garment* when they go on space walks. That's right, just like a baby!

You have more than 230 joints in your body.

An eyebrow hair lasts for only 10 weeks, whereas a hair can stay on your head for 5 years.

Some infections lead to *strawberry tongue*, in which the bumps on the tongue swell up, making it look like a strawberry.

Some of your muscles can contract and relax again in a fraction of a second, such as those in your eyes.

On average, right-handed people live 9 years longer than left-handed people!

You use 72 muscles when you talk. That's quite a workout!

The growing obesity problem has led to one British council installing bigger furnaces in its crematoriums that can hold 3-feet (1-meter) wide coffins.

Long, thin cell structures in your fingernails make them rip across, not downward.

Abnormal skin cells can be frozen away. Liquid nitrogen causes instant frostbite on healthy skin but is often used to get rid of warts and moles.

Men are more likely to be color-blind than women.

You're hairy all over! Only your lips, palms, and soles of your feet have no hair on them—the rest of your body is covered in about 5 million hairs.

Your heart beats more than 30 million times each year!

Your brain weighs half as much as your skin.

An Indian man sold one of his kidneys . . . to raise money for a trip to the 2007 World Cup Cricket match in the West Indies.

You have a stirrup, an anvil, and a hammer in each ear! They are tiny bones that were named in a time when there were more blacksmiths around than there are today.

> **Any part of your body can be removed and replaced with a machine except your brain.**

The lining of your stomach completely replaces itself every 3 days.

> **You lose 47 percent of your body's heat from your head. That's why you should wear a hat if it's chilly.**

You could live for a month without food but only a week without water.

The only animal that can get a sunburn, apart from a human, is a pig.

In ancient Greece, a prisoner called Histiaeus sent his son-in-law a secret message to start a rebellion . . . by tattooing it onto his slave's head!

Your thighbone, or *femur*, is the longest bone in your body.

Early American toothpaste boxes from 1968 were black and featured an x-ray picture of a decayed tooth. Marketing has improved a little since then!

You have 6 million *cones* in each eye! They are the cells that make you see colors.

The hormone that makes you grow is produced only when you sleep, so if you want to be taller, you should go to bed when you're told!

Long -distance swimmers eat while they're in the water to keep up their energy levels.

Women blink almost twice as much as men.

The ancient Greeks believed that a sneeze was a good sign from the gods. In parts of India, it's believed to be a sign of good health!

Fingernails grow four times more quickly than toenails.

Singer Screamin' Jay Hawkins was famous for a song called "Constipation Blues."

Each nerve cell in your brain can receive over 100,000 messages a second!

A Yemeni man was found to have four kidneys instead of two. Although he was offered money for his spare ones, he decided that they were a gift from Allah and kept all four.

A red blood cell takes less than a minute to go around your whole body!

Your hair grows more quickly in warm weather than in cold weather.

A New Zealand tree surgeon broke his leg near the top of a 130-foot (40-meter) high tree ... and was then injured further when the rescue helicopter swung him into another tree!

Your body is made up of 66 percent water.

There are 100,000 hairs on the average human head.

Babies and children blink less often than adults. Newborn babies blink only once or twice a minute!

Your lungs are different sizes! The left one is smaller to make room for your heart.

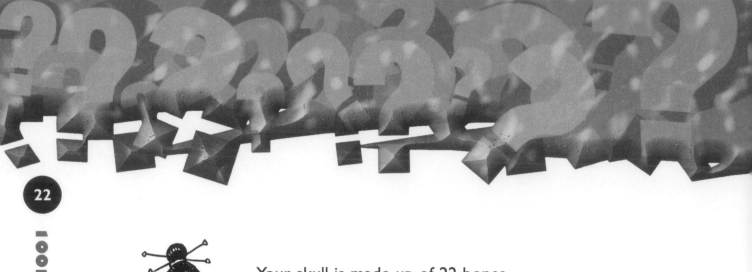

Your skull is made up of 22 bones.

A Chinese man has grown the nails on his left hand for 15 years, so that their total length is more than 3 feet (1 meter). He avoids crowded places in case one of them gets broken!

Japanese women have the highest average life span and can expect to live beyond the age of 80.

Children and young adults need twice as much oxygen as people over 80 years of age.

Your thyroid gland is butterfly shaped. It's in your neck and makes important substances that help you grow and develop properly.

Your gallbladder is dark green!

Someone who forgets a word or name during a conversation is suffering from *lethologica*.

Ever wondered what that little pink lump in the corner of your eye is? Our ancestors had an extra eyelid that would close horizontally to protect the eye. We haven't needed it for thousands of years, so it has disappeared through evolution.

More than half of your bones are in your hands and feet.

Brain cells are the only cells in the body that don't regenerate. When they're gone, they're gone!

A 1956 Olympic water polo match between Hungary and the Soviet Union was abandoned after it degenerated into an underwater brawl.

The skin is thickest on the soles of your feet and gets thicker if you walk around barefoot a lot. The skin is thinnest on your eyelids.

Every tiny move you make uses muscles—you have more than 630 altogether!

A hair follicle on your head will rest for up to 6 months after a hair falls out before a new hair sprouts out of it!

Ancient philosophers believed that mental activity took place in the heart.

Your brain was as big as an adult's when you were just 6 years old!

It's possible to live without your large intestine.

Your nose helps you to taste things! That's why it's difficult to taste your food if you have a cold and can't smell anything.

A Brazilian woman who had suffered from stomach pain for years was finally given an x-ray . . . which revealed a scalpel inside her body! The surgical tool had been left there 23 years earlier when she had given birth by cesarean section.

Dead bodies are stored in a morgue at a temperature of 35 to 39 degrees Fahrenheit (2 to 4 degrees Celsius).

Forensic scientists can identify a person's age, gender, race, and state of health from a single hair.

Gold can reduce swelling and is given to arthritis sufferers by injection.

A Dutch gym has naked workout sessions. Ewww!

Salivating before throwing up is the body's way of protecting your teeth from the high acid levels in vomit.

As you're reading this, 4 percent of your blood is in your heart. The rest is whizzing around your body!

An 80-year-old Chinese man agreed to have his hair washed for the first time in 23 years. It took 12 relatives and friends 5 hours to get all the grime out of his 6-foot (2-meter)-long matted locks, followed by his beard, which measured 5 feet (1.5 meters)!

The liver is your largest internal organ—it has more than 500 functions and has two blood supplies.

There are seven types of stool listed on the Bristol Stool Chart medical aid, ranging from "separate hard lumps, like nuts" (type 1), to "entirely liquid" (type 7).

The fingerprints of koala bears and humans are so similar that they could be confused at a crime scene.

You have an amazing nose! It's so sensitive that it can tell the difference between 10,000 smells.

You will walk the equivalent of five times around the world during your lifetime!

Nerve signals are super-fast! It takes less than 1/100th of a second for a nerve signal from your toe to reach your brain.

Women and children breathe more quickly than men.

A Polish car thief was tracked down after he left his false teeth at the crime scene! Police used dental records to catch the culprit.

The human body is at its lowest ebb between 3 a.m. and 4 a.m.— the most likely time for someone to die in their sleep.

The older you are, the more quickly your nails will grow.

Although they weigh a lot less, your bones are as strong as steel.

Even though your gastric juices are acidic enough to dissolve metal, you can't digest tomato seeds—they pass straight through your intestines.

Your largest muscles are the ones you sit on! You have a *gluteus maximus* in each buttock.

Ninety-nine percent of the body's calcium is in your bones and teeth.

Humans babies are born without kneecaps.

Laughing and coughing put more pressure on your spine than standing or walking do. Some people have even developed back injuries from coughing.

Your kidneys take just 4 minutes to clean all the blood in your body.

Touching the soft palate at the back of your mouth triggers a gag reflex, but this can be controlled with practice—sword swallowers train themselves to resist it.

Your small intestine is covered with tiny finger-like projections called *villi*. They increase the surface area of your intestine to absorb the maximum amount of nutrition from food.

Some of your muscles stretch to twice their resting length when you exercise!

When you cough, the air rushes through your windpipe faster than the speed of sound.

One in **600** people are born with *horseshoe kidney*, where the two kidneys have joined to make a horseshoe shape.

By the time you feel thirsty, your body is already dehydrated.

Humans have a tailbone! Its proper name is the *coccyx*, which means "cuckoo"—it got its name because it looks like a cuckoo's beak.

Your nails are naturally thick or thin—nothing can make them thicker, whatever the claims on nail cosmetics may say!

We are the only animals that cry tears when we are upset.

Eighty-five percent of people can curl their tongue into a tube. The other 15 percent get annoyed that they can't.

Your ears and nose keep growing throughout your whole life.

Poisons in the body can be stored in the hair shaft for years, even after death.

You have the same number of bones in your neck as a giraffe has. The difference is obvious...giraffe bones are a lot longer!

Your bones are alive! If they weren't full of living cells, they wouldn't be able to mend themselves when they break.

You lose your sense of smell as you get older, so children can smell far more than their parents or grandparents.

The nail on your middle finger grows more quickly than the others.

Surgeons trying to correct the limp of a 5-year-old boy in China lengthened the wrong leg! The confusion arose when the boy was anesthetized while lying on his back and operated on while lying on his stomach. Always best to check!

The deadly anthrax virus can live for years at room temperature. Luckily, it's not very common.

You spent the first half hour of your life as a single cell.

Your body is producing *cerebrospinal fluid* all the time! The fluid acts as a cushion to protect your brain and constantly needs replacing.

Babies less than 1 month old don't cry tears.

Hair and fingernails are made from the same substance, called *keratin*.

Synesthesia is a condition where two senses overlap. Russian artist Wassily Kandinsky, for example, perceived musical notes as colors.

A person with a cold sprays up to 40,000 infectious droplets into the air when he or she sneezes!

Identical twins have the same DNA but different fingerprints.

You are slightly taller in the morning than you are when you go to bed.

One type of E. coli causes food poisoning, but there are hundreds of strains of the bacteria—you have some in your intestine!

Professional athletes have a very slow resting heart rate.

Fatal insomnia is a rare inherited illness where sufferers get so little sleep that they eventually waste away and die.

The skull is much softer at birth to allow the brain to grow—newborn babies often have misshapen heads!

A lack of the mineral *iodine* in the diet causes a big lump in the neck when the thyroid gland swells up.

Your heart first started beating 3 weeks after you were conceived.

You dream for about 2 hours a night.

The US has the highest rate of obesity in the developed world—two-thirds of its adults are classed as overweight or obese.

Lung pinprick condition is a rare condition in which microscopic holes appear in the lungs.

Your muscles are made up of bundles of muscle fibers—each one is as thin as a hair.

March 8 is World Kidney Day . . . how will you celebrate?

Ten percent of people have a protruding belly button, or an *outie*. Whether you have an *innie* or an *outie* depends on the shape and size of your umbilical cord when you were born!

Fetuses sometimes have hiccups and also suck their thumbs . . . but probably not at the same time.

Your voice is unique! No two people have exactly the same larynx, nose, and mouth shape, so your voiceprint is all yours.

Your eye muscles work really hard—they make around 100,000 movements in a day.

Some people are born without an appendix. That saves them the trouble of having it out later . . .

Men have larger brains than women—but women have more brain cells!

The brain can't sense touch or pain, so brain surgery can be done while the patient is still awake! If a tumor is being removed, a surgeon may talk to the patient to check for alertness and to make sure that the operation is not damaging healthy parts of the brain.

You have water in your bones! Twenty percent of your skeleton is made up of water.

Doughnuts originally had a nut in the center.

Early bubble gum was pink because it was the only food coloring available at the time.

An Italian woman was cleaning the soil from potatoes for dinner when one turned out to be a hand grenade! Neighbors called the police, and the weapon was safely detonated.

Mice are a delicacy in Zambia and Malawi.

A New York restaurant offers the ultimate luxury pizza, topped with lobster and six kinds of caviar. It's a bargain at $1,000!

Boiling a lobster alive is a crime punishable by a fine in northern Italy.

Canadian sculptor Cosimo Cavallaro sprayed a whole house with ... cheese! He used 9,920 pounds (4,500 kilograms) of cheddar to cover the house inside and out.

African American scientist George W. Carver invented over 100 products made from peanuts, including cloth dyes and wood stains.

Sausages were invented thousands of years ago as a way of preserving and eating all the nasty-looking leftovers from slicing up an animal into cuts of meat.

Mexicans love chocolate sauce . . . on turkey!

Fifteenth-century candy canes weren't cane shaped but straight. Their curved shape came from a 17th-century priest who reshaped the candy so that it resembled shepherds' staffs.

If glacé cherries didn't have red coloring added, they would be beige.

The US is the world's largest producer of cheese.

During the 19th century, lard (pig fat) was used as a spread, like butter.

Vinegar eels are tiny worms that can be found in vinegar. Don't worry—bottled vinegar is pasteurized and filtered, so you won't find any wriggling around on your fish and chips!

The glue on Israeli postage stamps is certified kosher.

Japanese artist Tatsumi Orimoto goes around the world's cities and shakes hands with people . . . with baguettes strapped to his head, covering his face! He calls his performances *Bread Man*.

The mango comes from the same family as poison ivy—its skin can irritate the mouth if eaten.

Tea was originally a medicine in ancient China.

Witches' broom fungus and *frosty pod rot* are fungi that affect cacao plants, the plants used to make chocolate.

Welshman Captain Beany worships baked beans! He dresses in baked bean orange, bathes in beans, and formed the New Millennium Bean Party.

Tomatoes are berries.

A Mumbai businessman caused outrage when he opened the Hitler's Cross restaurant, where diners were greeted by a huge picture of the Nazi leader.

Black salt is actually pinkish gray!

You can't use fresh pineapple in a gelatin mold—it contains an enzyme that keeps it from setting.

Garlic has long been used for its medicinal properties and was an ancient Egyptian cure for worms and tumors.

More people are allergic to cows' milk than any other food.

Watermelons grow wild in the Kalahari Desert.

Marshmallow got its name from the plant of the same name. The first marshmallows contained the plant extract as its gelling agent, but modern forms use gelatin. This makes them unsuitable for vegetarians, since gelatin is made from boiled-up animal parts!

Poppy seeds contain the painkilling drug morphine and are banned in Singapore for this reason.

Carrot jam is a delicacy in Portugal.

Dried peas have been found in Egyptian tombs.

Grapefruits got their name from the way they grow in clusters, looking like bunches of huge grapes!

Dozens of people from northern India became fatally ill in 1998 after using what they thought was mustard oil in their cooking. It was discovered that the oil had been made from poisonous prickly poppy seeds, which look and taste like mustard seeds.

Black Magic and *Black Beauty* are types of eggplant.

A British girl put two store-bought organic eggs in an incubator to see if they would hatch. A few weeks later, two fluffy chicks popped out!

***Black Death* is the name of an Icelandic vodka.**

Turkeys originally came from Mexico. Their English name comes from the fact that they were first brought to England from Turkey.

Popcorn was discovered thousands of years ago by Native Americans, who enjoyed popcorn soup and popcorn beer.

Until the 18th century, English people believed tomatoes were poisonous.

Basil seed drink with honey is a thick, seed-filled Asian drink. Drinking it is said to be like drinking gluey masses of frogs' eggs!

Salad Blue and *Blue Congo* are types of potato. Anyone for blue fries?

Forbidden rice is a black rice grain that becomes dark purple when cooked and turns the water it is cooked in bright purple.

Drinking grapefruit juice can be dangerous when taking medication, since it allows chemicals to build up in the body.

Slices of bacon were known in the 16th century as *collops*. Christians would eat meat before Lent on Collop Monday.

The lovely smell of lemons can help you concentrate! A study using the citrus aroma in cars showed that both male and female drivers performed much better than they did without it.

Coca-Cola was originally green.

There are more than 350 different types of pasta.

The British are big tea fans—the average Brit drinks 23 times more tea than the average Italian!

Honey is antibacterial and never spoils.

It takes more calories to digest a piece of celery than there are in the celery itself. No point in eating that!

In the UK, 26 million eggs are eaten every day. That's an eggstraordinary amount!

Lens is Latin for *lentil*—the lenses in your eyes are lentil shaped!

A Chinese car dealer covered a Volkswagen Beetle in 440 pounds (200 kilograms) of chocolate for his Valentine's Day display!

Hedgehogs were eaten in medieval times and are still a source of food in some countries. One way to cook it is in clay—when the baked clay is broken off, the hedgehog spines come with it.

Popular Korean snack *beondegi* are silkworm pupae that have been steamed or boiled and then seasoned. They sound delicious!

The cucumber originally came from India.

A meal survey showed that the average Briton eats spaghetti bolognese 3,000 times in his or her lifetime.

Cashew nuts come from cashew apples!

Throwing celery onto the field is a tradition for fans of the English soccer team Chelsea. Even so, it has recently become a criminal offense, and one arrested fan vowed never to eat celery again!

The remains of 4,000-year-old noodles were found at a site in China in 2005, settling the argument of where they were invented!

There are more chickens in the world than any other bird.

Salt was highly prized by the Romans—soldiers were sometimes paid in salt which is how the word *salary* originated.

For one of his exhibitions, designer Jean-Paul Gaultier had dresses, shoes, and hats specially made . . . by bakers! His show was called *Pain Couture* and the exhibits were made from bread and pastry.

The first ketchup was made with pickled fish in East Asia.

During the Middle Ages, children were given beer for breakfast!

The average British household throws away almost a third of the food it buys.

A Welshman celebrated the opening of his new pizza takeout store by having a slice of ham and pineapple pizza tattooed on the back of his head! His tattoo took 3 hours, and the event raised money for charity.

Fruits with *choke* in their name are sour and difficult to swallow, such as the choke pear and chokecherry.

Watermelon rinds are edible and are used as a vegetable in Asian stir-fries and stews.

Brazil nuts grow only in rain forests.

An English fisherman saved an edible crab . . . because it had three claws! Instead of ending up as lunch, Claudette the mutant crustacean went on show at the local aquarium.

The first coffee was sold in pharmacies and was known as *Arabian wine.*

The Mount Horeb Museum in Wisconsin has a collection of over 4,000 different types of mustard.

A Chinese man fed instant noodles to his dogs too often—they became addicted and refused to eat anything else!

The largest chicken egg recorded had five yolks in it!

The tea in tea bags is the waste product left over from the sorting of higher-quality loose-leaf tea—it's known as *dust.*

There are no turkeys eaten in Turkey.

Japanese chocolate comes in fiery-hot *wasabi* flavor!

Until the 17th century, all carrots were purple. Now you can choose to eat orange, red, yellow, or white ones too!

> Roman Emperor Nero liked his iced desserts!
> He would send slaves to the mountains to fetch snow,
> which would then be mixed with fruit, nuts, and honey.

Chickpeas were used as a coffee substitute during World War I.

> A British man with a food phobia has lived mainly on cheese for 20 years. The only other thing he can bear to eat is potato chips!

Eggshells contain calcium and are sometimes used as a food additive.

Banana plants have been used to make cloth for hundreds of years in Japan.

Puffed rice is made from grains of rice that have been heated until they bubble up to produce thin outer walls. The noise you hear when you pour milk onto your cereal is those walls collapsing from the moisture!

Medieval church wafers were made with coats of arms imprinted on them.

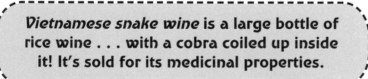

Vietnamese snake wine is a large bottle of rice wine . . . with a cobra coiled up inside it! It's sold for its medicinal properties.

In Poland and Germany, the last Thursday before Lent is known as *Fat Thursday*, when people stuff themselves with cakes!

Eggplant is so named because some types aren't purple but white, and as the fruits are growing, they look like eggs!

Until 2004, chewing gum was banned in Singapore.

A can of cola contains the equivalent of 7 teaspoons of sugar.

Former North Vietnamese president Ho Chi Minh once worked as a pastry assistant in the kitchens of London's Carlton Hotel.

Despite being a cancer-causing substance, talcum powder is still used in some countries to coat rice to improve its appearance. Talc-coated rice is banned in the US.

People train *pigtailed macaque monkeys* to collect coconuts in parts of Asia.

Peanut oil can be used to make paint, varnish, polish, insecticides, soap, and explosives.

Milk for US President William Taft and his family was provided by a cow that grazed freely on the White House lawn!

It takes 40 minutes to hard-boil an ostrich egg!

Until the 20th century, lobster was seen
as a food for the poor and was even used as fertilizer!

The poisonous plant *hemlock* has a large white root and can be mistaken for wild parsnip . . . with disastrous results!

A medieval Christmas dinner would consist of swan or peacock.

The Australian *finger lime* has the widest color variation of any citrus fruit—it can be green, red, orange, yellow, purple, black, or brown!

Garlic that has been stored in oil for too long can produce the highly toxic poison *botulism*.

Dogs have been eaten in China for thousands of years.

Trenchers were medieval plates made from stale bread. When the meal was finished, the trenchers would be given to the poor to eat. How generous!

Frost is necessary in the growing of parsnips. It helps to develop the flavor.

Bubble tea or *pearl tea* is an Asian tea drink that comes in different flavors. What makes it unusual is that it has big, black, chewy *tapioca* balls swimming around in it that lurk at the bottom of the cup!

The strawberry is the only fruit that has its seeds on its outer skin.

The Romans used to eat lettuce as a dessert.

The *horned melon*, also known as the *African horned cucumber*, has a jelly-like flesh that tastes like a cross between a cucumber and a kiwi fruit.

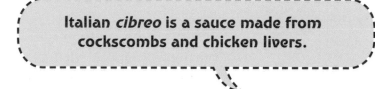

Italian *cibreo* is a sauce made from cockscombs and chicken livers.

French soups sold in the street were called *restaurers* for their restorative properties. The first restaurant opened in Paris in 1765, selling the soups and providing tables at which to eat them.

A rotten egg has a green yolk.

The amount of rice that rice *blast fungus* destroys each year could feed 60 million people.

China is the world's leading producer of apples.

Strawberries and red peppers both contain more vitamin C than oranges, weight for weight.

Snail-spitting champion Alan Jourden can spit a snail 31 feet (9.4 meters). Competitors run up before they spit out their mollusk as far as they can.

Peanuts are widely eaten in China and India, but peanut allergy is rare there.

Eggs 'n' brains is a southern US dish made with scrambled eggs and pig's brain. Yummy!

Before industrialized food production, one big noodle would be cooked for a meal in Chinese households—it was considered bad luck to cut it before it was served.

A *craisin* is a dried cranberry.

People in central Europe used to rub garlic on their chimneys and keyholes to keep away vampires and werewolves.

Cheese was invented in around 8000 BC.

Ancient Romans used to breed dormice (a type of rodent) for food. One dormouse made a tasty starter.

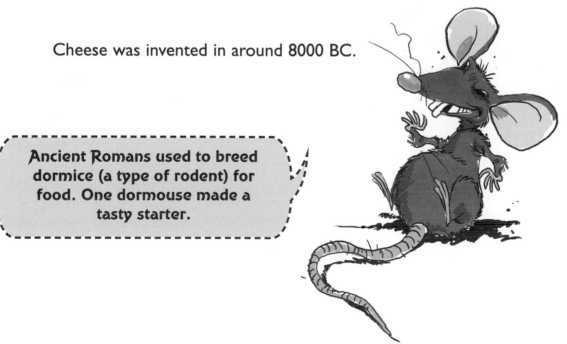

There are more Maltese people in Melbourne, Australia, than there are in Malta.

Guanciale is Italian cured pig's cheek.

White hens lay white eggs.

Some Indonesian men drink cobra blood to make them more manly. King cobra blood is the most expensive!

Coffee was originally banned in some countries because it was considered addictive.

The first cheesecakes were served at the ancient Greek Olympic games more than 2,000 years ago.

Ninety percent of Cambodia's agricultural land is used to grow rice.

The *turpentine mango* smells of . . . turpentine! It's safe to eat, but the experience is said to be like eating a regular mango in a freshly painted room.

Nineteenth-century English geologist William Buckland claimed to have eaten his way through the animal kingdom, including panther and crocodile. He said the worst things he had tasted were mole and Portuguese man-of-war jellyfish.

No species other than humans drink milk from the mothers of other species.

Eating large amounts of carrots will turn your skin orange.

It takes 40 liters (88 pints) of sap from a maple tree to make 1 liter (2.2 pints) of maple syrup.

Artist Gayle Chong Kwan has made sculptured landscapes from food. Her works have included puffed rice walls, mashed potato mountains, cheese buildings, and a ham tower.

Chicken neck skin is sometimes used as a casing for kosher sausages.

Abbeville, Louisiana, has a Giant Omelet Celebration in which a 5,000-egg omelet is made in a giant pan.

Sliced bread was invented in 1928 in Missouri.

Candy canes first became peppermint flavored with red and white stripes in Sweden in the 19th century.

A *fuzzy melon* is an Asian vegetable similar to squash.

Kangaroo meat is very low in fat— kangaroo sausages, known as *kanga bangas*, and kangaroo steaks are available in Australia.

Japanese scientists believe chewing gum is good for your brain. Chewing stimulates the learning center of the brain and can actually improve your memory!

A chicken can lay more than 200 eggs a year.

The early Catholic Church banned sausages since they were traditionally eaten during pagan festivals.

Fortune cookies were invented in California.

Fried cod tongues are a popular Norwegian dish.

Ankimo is a Japanese delicacy of steamed monkfish liver with the veins removed.

There is no ham in a hamburger. The name comes from the fact that the first meat patties served in a bread bun were made in Hamburg, Germany.

Unbelievable Animal Facts

A woodpecker's tongue can be as long as its body! It has a barb on the end of it for skewering grubs. Yummy!

Insects first appeared 300 million years ago, even farther back in time than dinosaurs.

Large rodents called agoutis are the only animals that can open brazil nuts with their teeth.

Locusts can fly for 20 hours without stopping.

The *mimic* octopus can change its shape and color to look like other sea creatures. It can even make itself long and thin to do an impression of a sea snake!

The eyes of a hamster blink independently of each other.

Osedax mucofloris is a slimy sea worm that feeds on whale remains and looks like a flower growing from the bone it's eating. Its name means "bone-eating mucus flower!"

A flamingo always feeds with its head upside down.

Austrians were puzzled when they found a dead shark on a freshwater riverbank. A chef eventually confessed—he had put it there as a joke when it began to smell as he defrosted it for a buffet!

Meerkats are immune to many deadly venoms and will eat scorpions . . . stinger and all!

A New Zealand fisherman caught a colossal squid that was 30 feet (10 meters) long. Its body was so enormous that *calamari rings* (squid rings) made from it would be as big as tractor tires!

The US and Russian armies have trained dolphins to rescue lost divers and seek out underwater mines.

It can take a month for the contents of a sloth's stomach to digest completely.

A giant anteater gobbles up about 3,000 ants and termites in 1 day, using its sticky tongue that can be as long as 2 feet (60 centimeters)!

Beavers have a set of transparent eyelids to protect their eyes as they swim underwater.

Some fish can walk! Mudskippers can survive on land and have strong fins that they use as legs to get around.

The strongest leather comes from ostrich skin.

Workers at a Kenyan animal sanctuary were surprised when an orphaned baby hippo chose Mzee the 130-year-old giant tortoise as its new parent! Since Owen the hippo was rescued from the sea after the 2004 tsunami, the pair have lived, slept, and played together.

Chemicals taken from *Kamchatka* crabs have been used to treat burns.

In the same way that people are right- or left-handed, elephants are right- or left-tusked!

The burrowing owl makes its nest underground and lines it with cow dung.

Staff at a British zoo had to hand-feed milk to a baby *colobus monkey* after it was rejected by its mother . . . for having hiccups!

Polar bears have transparent (not white!) hair, and their skin is black to absorb maximum heat from the sun.

Hippos, whales, and dolphins are the only mammals that give birth underwater.

Bees have five eyes!

Birds can eat berries that are highly poisonous to humans.

Fuji the dolphin put on weight after having her diseased tail amputated because she couldn't swim properly. Handlers at the Japanese aquarium came up with a speedy solution—a new tail was made from the material used for Formula-1 racing car tires!

The total combined weight of the world's ant population is heavier than the weight of the human population.

The greater bulldog bat likes to go fishing! Its super-sonar detects the slightest of ripples then it swoops down to catch the fish with its feet!

More than 40 percent of all mammal species are rodents.

Both male and female octopuses die shortly after mating.

1001 Unbelievable Facts

Dachshund means "badger dog": the dogs were originally bred for killing badgers, rabbits and foxes. Not so cute after all!

Snakes have no taste buds.

The only fruit eaten by aardvarks is known as the *aardvark cucumber*. African bushmen call it *aardvark dung*!

Dalmatians are genetically disposed toward deafness. Until this was discovered, they were thought to be plain stupid!

Frogs don't drink water, they absorb it through their skin.

A stag's antlers are made of bone.

An elephant's stomach makes lots of noise when it's digesting food, so elephants can stop their digestion at will if there's any danger of a predator hearing it!

Mexican police discovered 132 wild animals in the trunk of a bus after investigating strange noises. Some toucans, iguanas, parrots, snakes and turtles were confiscated, but none of the passengers would admit to owning them. So no arrests were made!

Chalkbrood is a fungal disease that destroys honeybee larvae and gives them a chalky white appearance.

Owls are farsighted, so they can't see things close up very clearly.

Austrian mechanics soon discovered the cause of a squeak in a tourist's car: a kitten trapped above one of the wheels! The kitten was shaken but had survived the car's 900-mile (1,500-kilometer) journey.

Adult swordfish have no teeth.

Squirrels can climb trees faster than they can run on the ground!

An armadillo can stay underwater for up to 6 minutes! First it fills its stomach with air; otherwise it would sink under the weight of its heavy body armor.

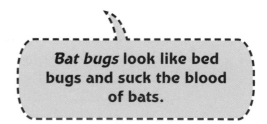

Bat bugs look like bed bugs and suck the blood of bats.

A male *Kodiak* bear on its hind legs is gigantic: over 10 feet (3 meters) tall.

A pair of storks made a nest in the middle of a German golf course and filled it with golf balls. They're probably still waiting for them to hatch!

Newborn rattlesnakes have no rattle! The bead needed to make the rattle noise in their tail doesn't form until they have shed their first skin.

Some starfish are circular. They must feel a little out of place . . .

Crabeater seals don't eat crabs! They eat *krill*, tiny shrimp-like creatures.

Until 1997, the punishment for killing a panda in China was death.

1001 Unbelievable Facts

A giant catfish frightened divers in a Dutch vacation park. The monster fish was found to be 7 feet 6 inches (2.3 meters) long and ate three ducks a day, but staff promised that it wouldn't eat people!

A spider monkey's tail is so strong that it can pick fruit with it!

Bedbugs and fleas can live for a whole year without eating.

The African pygmy mouse gets water by stacking pebbles in front of its burrow and drinking the dew from them in the morning.

Pigs don't sweat. They roll around in mud to keep cool in hot weather!

The African pancake tortoise has a flat, soft shell . . . just like a pancake! The shell is no use against predators, but it does help the tortoise to avoid them by enabling it to hide in narrow crevices.

Both the coat and the skin of a tiger are stripy.

Birds' eyes are fixed in their sockets, so they have to move their whole head to look at something—try it yourself, keeping your eyes still!

The color of a flamingo comes from all the shrimp it eats. A pale flamingo isn't getting enough food!

The male four-horned antelope is the only mammal with four horns.

When unraveled, the thread of a single silkworm's cocoon can be over half a mile (1 kilometer) long.

Two smelly musk hogs were married in a lavish ceremony in Taiwan to celebrate the Year of the Pig. The pigs were dressed up for the occasion and even got to eat some wedding cake!

A queen termite can live for 15 years.

The roadrunner is a type of cuckoo. Some Native American tribes believed that it protected against evil spirits.

Lions are color-blind— that's why a zebra's camouflage is so effective!

A German farmer found a novel way of protecting his sheep from hoof infection: he dressed his flock in special little rubber boots!

Male lions spend most of their time resting and are inactive for about 20 hours a day.

A seal was found over 4 miles (6 kilometers) from the sea, struggling down a country lane in Lancashire, England. How it got there is still a mystery!

Elephants have only four teeth that can be replaced up to six times in their lifetime.

The colorful St. Andrew's Cross spider is so called because it rests in its web with its legs outstretched in an X formation.

Sharks are covered in sharp, tooth-like scales called *denticles*.

The tapir has a long snout that is *prehensile*—that means it can move in all directions and grasp things!

The harpy eagle is so large and powerful that it can easily carry away a monkey in its talons.

Phonetics experts have discovered that birds chirp with regional accents!

The call of a blue whale is louder than a jumbo jet and can be heard 500 miles (800 kilometers) away.

A cat's nose has a unique print, just as your fingerprints do!

A group of owls is known as a *parliament*.

If a shark is turned upside down, it will go into a state of paralysis, known as *tonic immobility*, for up to 15 minutes.

Tarantulas can't spin webs.

An elderly Swedish woman took animal rescue a little too far: police found that she had been sheltering 11 swans in her tiny Stockholm apartment for more than 5 years!

Snakes are an example of *obligate carnivores*: all they eat is meat, meat, and more meat!

There are 18 different kinds of piranha fish, but only four of them are dangerous.

Unlike other big cats, cheetahs can't roar. They can purr, though!

A rat can go without water for longer than a camel.

If you find a *mermaid's purse* washed up on the beach, it's the empty egg case of a dogfish, skate, or maybe even a shark!

A tiny tree frog wandered into the freezer of a café in Darwin, Australia, and was found frozen solid. Once thawed out, though, it was fine. (Maybe it had only gone in for a croaka-cola . . .)

West African woolly bats are so tiny that they live in spiderwebs.

Amphibian skin absorbs chemicals in addition to water, so a frog sitting in an anesthetic solution will quickly go to sleep.

A German cat was sent through the mail after sneaking into a parcel while its owner looked for more tape.

Brazilian police went to investigate an abandoned truck and discovered five lions inside it! Each of the lions had to be fed 22 pounds (10 kilograms) of meat a day until their owner could be found.

Snails can sleep for 3 years.

The postman caterpillar eats poisonous leaves. It feeds on cyanide-filled passionflower leaves and stores the poison in its spikes to put off predators.

Big, fat atlas beetle larvae can bite when touched.

Sea urchins have been on the planet for about 450 million years.

A new bakery that opened near Frankfurt, Germany, offered treats such as tuna cakes and garlic cookies . . . just for dogs!

The 200 cats brought to a Chinese village to get rid of the rat problem were rewarded for their hard work with an enormous fish banquet!

No two zebras have the same stripy pattern.

A cow that lost part of her leg when she broke it in a fall was saved from slaughter when her owner had a false one made. Now she can move fine!

A parrot fish's teeth continue to grow throughout its life.

The platypus and the echidna are the only two mammals that lay eggs and give their young milk.

One pat of elephant dung can contain up to 7,000 dung beetles!

Cats hate the smell of oranges and lemons.

A North American *caribou* deer will travel up to 3,000 miles (5,000 kilometers) in a year.

Giant clamshells are so big that in the past, they have been used as children's baths and church fonts.

Sea pigs are a type of sea cucumber: they live in really deep oceans, rolling around in the mud on the seabed and eating it!

Pandas can't digest bamboo very well, but they still spend all day eating it—98 percent of what they eat is bamboo!

A male African elephant weighs as much as 170 men.

An oyster can be male one year and female the next!

An Australian crocodile was so annoyed by the sound of a chain saw nearby that it ran at the man using it and grabbed it from him!

A rhinoceros's horn isn't a true horn—it's made of matted hair.

Whales have been found with circular scars on their skin—marks from the suckers of giant squid.

The coconut crab, or robber crab, lives on land and will drown in water.

Giraffes, camels, and cats are the only animals that walk by moving both their left feet together, then both their right feet together.

Some shrews have red teeth! The strange color comes from iron deposits.

Swordfish have special organs in their heads that heat up their eyes and brain.

A cow caused an accident by wandering into a road in Colombia and was punished by being put in prison.

Owls can't turn their heads completely around. They can turn them farther than you can, though—to an angle of 135 degrees in each direction.

Some horses are allergic to grass! Their eyes water when they eat it, just like the eyes of a person with hayfever when exposed to ragweed pollen.

Pandas have unusual paws that look like hands with a thumb and five fingers on each.

The *tarantula hawk* is actually a wasp! The female attacks and paralyzes a tarantula so that she can lay her egg on its body. The hatched larva then eats the tarantula alive.

The powerful jaws and sharp teeth of a snapping turtle can rip off a person's finger.

King snakes, such as the king cobra, eat other snakes.

A cat's heart beats twice as fast as a human's!

A rare armadillo in Argentina is small and pink—its name is the *pink fairy armadillo*!

Rodents are immune to the rabies virus.

If it has no food, a ribbon worm can eat up to 95 percent of its own body to survive.

An adult mayfly lives for only 1 day. It doesn't even get a chance to eat anything since it spends all its time mating and laying eggs.

Siberian huskies can live and work in temperatures as low as minus 75 degrees Fahrenheit (minus 60 degrees Celsius).

Parrot fish can make themselves a kind of mucus sleeping bag! It masks their smell from predators and keeps parasites away.

Not all penguins live in cold climates—the Galápagos penguin lives near the equator.

Pit vipers are so called because of the holes between their nostrils and eyes that contain heat sensors. They track down prey in the dark by detecting the difference in temperature between an animal and its background. The sensitive heat detectors can pick up a difference in temperature of less than 33.8 degrees Fahrenheit (1 degree Celsius)!

Pea crabs are tiny crabs—the size of peas, in fact!

Black bears have been known to take the lids off jars and undo door latches.

Giant sea stars are starfish that can have an arm span of more than 24 inches (60 centimeters)! They can be brown, green, red, or orange.

Odd-eyed cats have one eye that is blue and one eye that is green, orange, or yellow.

Sloths eat, sleep, and give birth upside down. They are held in place by their sharp claws and will even stay hanging from a branch after they have died!

Penguins have a filter above their eyes that converts saltwater to freshwater. The excess brine drips out of their bills, and sometimes they sneeze it out!

A starving mouse will eat its own tail.

Dolphins have no sense of smell. They can see and hear very well, though.

The honey possum is a tiny Australian marsupial that is half the size of a mouse and feeds entirely on pollen and nectar.

Basenji dogs have unusually shaped larynxes and don't bark— they make a yodeling sound!

A shark's liver makes up around a quarter of its body mass. It's so huge because it provides the buoyancy that other fish get from gas-filled swim bladders.

Anteaters are the only mammals that have no teeth.

A four-legged duckling was born on a duck farm in Hampshire, England. The farm owner named him Stumpy.

When it attacks prey, the great white shark rolls its eyes backward to protect them.

If you gently scratch a koala's fur, your fingers will smell of eucalyptus—their favorite food!

The fierce grasshopper mouse will defend its territory by howling like a little wolf!

At twilight, hundreds of thousands of bats fly out of Carlsbad Caverns in New Mexico. They form a dense whirlwind but none of the bats ever hit each other.

Unbelievable History Facts

Nineteenth-century British prime minister William Gladstone was once injured in an attack by a cow during a country walk.

In ancient Greece, it was forbidden to eat shark meat at women's festivals.

The remains of Louis IX of France are in more than one place: some of his entrails were buried where he died in Tunis, in North Africa; others are in Palermo, Italy; and one of his fingers is in Paris. The rest of his body disappeared in the 16th century.

Richard I of England (also known as Richard the Lionheart) died from an arrow wound that became gangrenous.

The murder rate in the Middle Ages was about 10 times higher than it is today.

Before coins were invented, shells were used in many countries as money.

The *Slinky* toy was invented in the early 1940s after US engineer Richard James dropped a torsion spring and thought its movements were fun!

One of the first glues was made by the ancient Egyptians . . . from boiled-up animal skins!

The first factory-produced toilet paper became available in 1857 in the US. People used all sorts of things before that—anything from leaves and fruit skins for the poor to lace or wool for the rich!

The first five Tarzan films were silent. No Tarzan calls in those . . .

Nelson Mandela's first name was Rolihlahla, but his teacher couldn't pronounce it and chose Nelson for him instead, after Horatio Nelson.

Arctic explorer John Hornby died of starvation after trying to spend a year without supplies by the Thelon River, in Canada.

The 3-mile (5-kilometer)-long tomb of Chinese emperor Qin Shi Huangdi contains more than 8,000 life-size clay soldiers, created 2,300 years ago to protect him in the afterlife.

The ancient Egyptians were the first to establish a 365-day year.

Gustave Eiffel originally intended to build his famous tower in Barcelona for the 1888 Universal Exposition, but his idea was rejected.

The tug-of-war was an Olympic Games event between 1900 and 1920.

Fourteenth-century traveler John Mandeville wrote that the cotton plant "was a wonderful tree which bore tiny lambs on the ends of its branches"!

Ancient Egyptians shaved their heads to stay cool in the heat and to keep from getting lice.

Many 19th-century artists and writers living in Paris were fond of a green alcoholic drink called *absinthe*, also known as "the green fairy." It was believed to be dangerously addictive and cause madness and so was banned in most countries by 1915.

The *Titanic* sank in 1912, but its wreck wasn't discovered until 1985.

Charlie Chaplin anonymously entered a Charlie Chaplin look-alike competition and didn't win any prizes at all!

The careers of many stars of silent movies collapsed with the arrival of "talkies"—movies with sound.

Furnaces beneath the floors of buildings provided central-heating systems in ancient times.

Leo II became the Byzantine emperor in 474 when he was just 7 years old!

Jimmy Carter was the first US president to be born in a hospital.

During the Ming dynasty, important officials wore belt buckles carved from the beaks of hornbill birds.

The first man on the moon, Neil Armstrong, got carsick as a child.

New Zealand mountaineer Sir Edmund Hillary spent his early adulthood as a beekeeper.

A popular form of art in medieval Russia was the carving of walrus tusks.

Christopher Columbus wasn't the first European explorer to reach the Americas. Vikings had landed in Canada in the 10th or 11th century.

Mozart wrote his first piece of music when he was just 5 years old.

Clipperton Island, in the east Pacific Ocean, is a ring-shaped island with a lagoon in the middle that was named after an 18th-century pirate.

The *lyre* was an ancient Greek musical instrument made from a tortoiseshell and some antelope horns.

Neither of Joseph Haydn's parents could read music. That didn't stop him from becoming one of the world's most famous composers!

Vikings drank from the skulls of their defeated enemies.

In 1863, a naughty boy called Santiago Ramóny Cajal was locked up for destroying his town's main gate with his homemade cannon. He went on to become a top scientist!

The Chinese invented fireworks more than 2,000 years ago. The sound was created to scare off evil spirits.

Deer antlers were used in the Stone Age to make harpoons, axes, combs, and needles.

Popes normally wear a tiara made from gold or silver for their coronation, but in 1800, Pope Pius VII had to wear one made from papier-maché! The French Republicans had just stolen all the good ones.

The mummy of Siptah showed that the young Egyptian ruler had a severely deformed foot.

Ernest Hemingway had a cat with six toes.

Before high-speed drills were invented, dentists used slow hand drills on their patients' teeth. Ouch!

Native American tepees were originally made from animal skins.

The bullet that killed Admiral Horatio Nelson is on display in Windsor Castle, England.

The hair from a young Roman's first shave would be offered to the gods. Emperor Nero put his in a lovely gold box with some pearls!

French artist Henri de Toulouse Lautrec broke both his legs in his early teens and they stopped growing. As an adult, he had a fully grown torso and child's legs.

Surveyor J. G. Tierney drowned while looking for a suitable site for the Hoover Dam on the Nevada-Arizona border. Exactly 13 years later, his son died in a fall at the construction site of the dam.

Construction of Barcelona's unique *Sagrada Familia* church began in 1883, and it still isn't finished! Work is due to be completed in 2026.

During World War II, no Olympic Games were held.

Ancient Chinese coins were rectangular with a hole in the middle. The hole was for stringing them together.

India hasn't invaded another country in the last 10,000 years of history.

The first helicopter flight lasted 20 seconds, with the rotary wing aircraft managing to get 1 foot (30 centimeters) off the ground!

12 million Africans were taken to the Americas before the slave trade was banned in 1808.

Within the space of 77 years, the Russian city of St. Petersburg had its name changed to Petrograd, then Leningrad, then back to St. Petersburg again.

The owl was a symbol of death for the Aztecs, Mayans, and ancient Romans.

Dr. Mary Edwards Walker became the first female US Army surgeon in 1863. She went on to fight for women's dress reform and was arrested several times for wearing men's clothing.

Early concrete was made with volcanic ash.

Some ancient tribes used animal dung to stiffen their hair. And you thought gel was stinky!

Legendary American Olympic gold medalist Jesse Owens died of lung cancer after smoking for 35 years.

All of Queen Anne of Great Britain's 18 children died before the age of 12.

Sunglasses were worn in China as long ago as the 12th century, with pieces of smoky quartz used as dark lenses. They were worn more to conceal facial expressions during interrogation than for protection against the sun!

Alexander the Great ordered his soldiers to shave off their beards in case the enemy used them as a handle to grab hold of!

Marilyn Monroe worked in an airplane parts factory before she became famous.

US President Woodrow Wilson's wife, Edith, was a descendent of Native American Pocahontas.

The FA Cup is the oldest soccer competition. The first final was in 1872 between teams called the Wanderers and the Royal Engineers. The Wanderers won 1–0!

Nineteenth-century French writer Guy de Maupassant disliked the Eiffel Tower so much that he would often have lunch in its restaurant . . . so he wouldn't have to look at it!

The Volkswagen *Beetle* car was designed for Adolf Hitler by Ferdinand Porsche.

The sister ship of the *Titanic* was to be called *Gigantic*, but its name was changed to *Britannic* after the disaster involving the first ship. *Britannic* sank too after hitting a mine in 1916.

In ancient times, children were considered to be grown-ups around the age of 12. They were expected to give up any toys to the gods.

King Henry VIII's first wife was chosen for him when he was 11 years old, following his brother's death. He was to marry his brother's widow when he was old enough.

French aviator Henri Fabre made the first seaplane in 1910. The strange invention flew tail-first and was called *Le Canard*—The Duck!

US President William Howard Taft was a big man. So big, in fact, that he kept getting stuck in the White House bathtub and a larger one had to be installed.

Until the 18th century, it was considered unmanly to eat with a fork.

Winston Churchill was born in a ladies' room in Blenheim Palace when his mother went into labor during a dance.

Argentina was named in the 16th century. The country is rich in silver, so the name came from the Latin for silver, *argentum*.

Hollywood icon James Dean starred in only three films. Tragically, he died in a car crash at age 24.

Beer is one of the oldest drinks and was even enjoyed by the ancient Egyptians!

Ancient anatomists believed that the arteries transported air through the body. Blood pools in the veins after death, so the arteries of a corpse seem empty.

Alan Shepard was the first astronaut to play golf on the moon.

Champagne was invented by a merry French monk!

The shape of a pyramid represents the rays of the sun falling to Earth. The step formation was designed so that the dead pharaoh inside could walk up to heaven on the sun rays!

Murderous dictator Idi Amin gave himself the snappy title "His Excellency President for Life, Field Marshal Al Hadji, Dr Idi Amin, VC (Victoria Cross) , DSO, MC, Lord of All the Beasts of the Earth and Fishes of the Sea, and Conqueror of the British Empire in Africa in General and Uganda in Particular."

The first elevator shaft was invented 4 years before the elevator!

African American Rosa Parks started a mass civil rights movement in 1955 when she was arrested for refusing to give up her bus seat to a white man.

Greek fire was a weapon used by the Byzantine Greeks in naval battles. A stream of burning fluid that couldn't be put out with water was fired at enemy ships.

In 1893, New Zealand became the first country to allow all its women to vote.

Only 48 hat tricks (scoring three times) have been scored throughout the FIFA World Cup's history. None were scored during the 2006 tournament, but eight were scored in 1954!

The lead in pencils was never really lead! Pencils were developed from graphite sticks, which were used in the 16th century to mark sheep, and the first ones had casings made from string or sheepskin.

The Romans built 53,000 miles (85,000 kilometers) of roads across their empire. That's a lot of digging!

The first hard hat was known as a "hard-boiled hat" and was made from canvas hardened with glue and black paint.

The 1938 radio broadcast of H. G. Wells's *The War of the Worlds* caused panic among many listeners who believed that aliens really had landed!

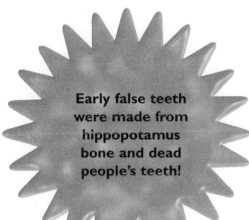

Early false teeth were made from hippopotamus bone and dead people's teeth!

John F. Kennedy could read so quickly that he often got through two or three books a day. He could speak quickly too and held the record for fastest public speaker.

Soviet cosmonaut Valentina Tereshkova was the first woman in space in 1963, but it was another 19 years before the Russians allowed another woman to fly up there!

The first affordable car, the Ford Model T, had a top speed of 45 miles (72 kilometers) per hour and worked with a single pedal.

Nineteenth-century Scottish explorer James Augustus Grant suffered severe swelling to his leg while in Africa and was given a hot poultice made from cow dung, salt, and mud from the lake. It would have taken his mind off the pain, if nothing else!

Viking celebratory feasts could last for 10 days!

Wealthy ancient Egyptians were embalmed in honey when they died.

The fire that started after the 1906 San Francisco earthquake caused more damage than the earthquake itself did.

The Boab Prison Tree is a huge, hollow tree that was used to lock up prisoners on their way to Derby, Australia, during the 19th century.

Seventy nations were involved in World War II.

When the nudes in Michelangelo's Sistine Chapel paintings were considered too shocking, another artist was asked to paint clothes over the offending parts!

St. Paul's Cathedral in London has been built and rebuilt at least five times.

Sixteenth-century aristocrat Lucrezia Borgia had a hollow ring that stored poison for use in her enemies' drinks.

Ancient Greek engineer Archimedes invented the first luxury ship in the 3rd century BC. Large enough to carry 600 people, it had a garden, a temple, and even a gym!

J. R. R. Tolkien's *Lord of the Rings* trilogy took 12 years to write. Tolkien's day job was as an Oxford University professor.

Frederick the Great preferred the company of his greyhounds to people and wanted to be buried next to them when he died. His successor, Frederick William II, was having none of it and had himself buried next to his father!

Lightning struck the Eiffel Tower in 1902, damaging the monument's top 328 feet (100 meters).

Victorian mailmen in England wore red tunics and were known as robins.

The best-known Tarzan actor, Johnny Weissmuller, was an Olympic-gold-medal-winning swimmer and set 67 world records in swimming during the 1920s.

Chauvet Cave in southern France contains cave paintings that are more than 30,000 years old.

The remains of Christopher Columbus started off in Valladolid, Spain, and were moved several times to Seville, Santo Domingo, in the Dominican Republic, Havana, in Cuba, and back to Seville again!

British prime minister Lord Palmerston was often late for appointments—even dinner with Queen Victoria!

Ancient Greek perfume containers were such shapes as helmets and sandaled feet. Today's perfume bottles are a little more romantic!

Seventeenth-century aristocrat Prince Rupert of the Rhine took his large poodle into battle with him on several occasions.

People only began to celebrate Christmas more than 400 years after Jesus Christ died. Later, under Oliver Cromwell, it was made illegal for more than a decade.

Seventeenth-century bottles of champagne exploded so frequently that cellar workers had to wear iron masks for protection.

The Tower of Pisa took 174 years to build, and it was never even straight to begin with!

Nineteenth-century American poet Emily Dickinson wrote more than 1,700 poems, but fewer than a dozen were published in her lifetime.

The waxy-looking embalmed body of Soviet leader Vladimir Lenin has been on display in Red Square since he died in 1924.

The first living beings to go up in a hot air balloon were a sheep, a duck, and a rooster in 1783.

Heavy snow slowed down the normally accurate Big Ben clock in London on New Year's Eve in 1962, making it announce the new year 10 minutes late.

Henry VIII decided that because she couldn't give him a son, his second wife, Anne Boleyn, must be a witch!

Polish American pianist Józef Hofmann had such small hands that he had to use a specially made piano with narrow keys.

Until 1984, no television programs were broadcast during the month of July in Iceland. What on earth did they do instead?

French novelist Victor Hugo also produced more than 4,000 drawings in his lifetime, sometimes using coffee or soot.

Gerald Ford was the longest-living US president, living to the age of 93 years, 165 days.

The first ever newspaper was printed in 1605 and looked like a book.

Can openers were invented 50 years after tin cans.

The Nobel Peace Prize is named after Swedish chemist Alfred Nobel—the man who invented dynamite.

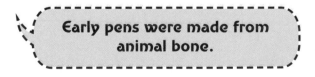

Early pens were made from animal bone.

A steeplejack did a parachute jump from the top of New York's Statue of Liberty in 1912.

American inventor Thomas Edison proposed to his wife in Morse code!

Levi Strauss invented jeans in the 1850s when he saw a need for long-lasting pants among miners. His first versions were made with sailcloth, then he imported a French material called *serge de Nimes* . . . which became shortened to *denim*.

The first Mercedes car was named after a company executive's daughter.

Even ancient Greek babies had rattles—hollow clay shapes had bits of clay inside to make the rattle sound.

Louis XIV became king of France at the age of 4 and went on to reign for 72 years.

Mystery surrounds the death of American writer Edgar Allan Poe—he was found wandering the streets in a delirious state, wearing someone else's clothes, and died shortly afterward.

The first job of British naturalist and explorer Alfred Wallace was as a builder.

The name Wendy wasn't used before the publication of J. M. Barrie's *Peter Pan*.

Italian composer Antonio Vivaldi started off as a violin teacher and was once fired from his job!

Alfred Nobel's studies on explosives tragically caused the death of his brother Emil in an explosion.

American astronaut Buzz Aldrin's mother's maiden name was Moon.

Yellow tennis balls weren't used at Wimbledon until 1986. Before that, they were white.

Sugar Ray Robinson was one of the greatest boxers of all time, winning his first 40 fights as a professional.

Danish physicist Niels Bohr made his escape from the Nazis in 1943 in a fishing boat.

The first lighthouse was built in 285 BC near Alexandria, Egypt. The light was created by a fire that had to be kept burning all night!

Nelson Mandela was the oldest elected president of South Africa, taking office at the age of 75.

Five workers died during the construction of the Empire State Building in New York City.

Viking coins were valued for their weight. If a Viking had to pay less for something, he would clip a bit off his coin!

Christmas 2004 was the first white Christmas in New Orleans, Louisiana, for 50 years.

Unbelievable Science Facts

Brazil nut trees can live for more than 500 years.

A bolt of lightning is so hot that if it hits sand, it can turn it into glass!

A trillion metric tons of the world's water evaporates each day in the sun. Luckily, it all comes down again when it rains!

Scientists have created rice that contains human genes! Genetically modified rice was developed with a human liver gene and, more recently, saliva and breast milk proteins.

Dust from Africa and China can end up in North America, carried across the sea by trade winds.

Only one in 1,000 oysters contains a pearl.

Italian astronomer Galileo Galilei was arrested for claiming that the sun was the center of the universe. His books were also banned by the Catholic Church.

The jumping spider doesn't use big muscles to jump! The energy needed is instead created by a kind of hydraulic system that changes the pressure of its blood and quickly stiffens the legs.

Water is the only substance that occurs naturally in liquid, solid, and gas forms (water, ice, and steam).

The supersonic airliner Concorde could fly around the world in 31 hours, 27 minutes.

Earth isn't completely spherical! It bulges in the middle—if you take a ball and squash it slightly from top to bottom, that is the shape of our planet.

The coldest temperature ever measured on Earth was minus 129 Fahrenheit (minus 89 Celsius) at Vostok, Antarctica, on July 21, 1983.

Liquid oxygen is sky blue.

Silver has antimicrobial properties and was used in many treatments before the invention of antibiotics. People would often put a silver coin in their milk to keep it from going sour!

A freak summer hailstorm left Australian capital Canberra under a blanket of ice. In some parts of the city, the ice was up to 3 feet (1 meter) deep!

The Atlantic Ocean is increasing in width by 1 inch (3 centimeters) every year.

The gravity on Mars is less than 40 percent of that on Earth. That means that if you could stand on Mars, you would weigh much less than you do now—instant weight loss!

Scottish biologist Alexander Fleming used multicolored bacteria to create germ paintings! The bacteria were invisible as he painted but became colorful as they grew.

The sun is 4.5 billion years old.

Rain forests cover only 2 percent of the world's surface, but more than 50 percent of all our plants and animals are found there.

The largest part of an iceberg is hidden beneath the sea's surface.

Research has shown that deadly puffer fish poison contains cancer-fighting properties and may be used in future treatments.

A hurricane the size of Earth has been raging on Jupiter for the past 300 years!

There's no such thing as moonlight! The light you see is the reflection of sunlight off the moon's surface.

Before the birth of the word 'scientist' in 1833, scientists were known as *natural philosophers* or *men of science*. (Women got pretty much left out back then!)

Mussels, as well as oysters, produce pearls.

The paper for US dollar bills is made from cotton.

There have been no cases of the deadly smallpox virus since 1978, but cultures of the virus are held at the Centers for Disease Control and Prevention in the US and at the Institute of Virus Preparations in Siberia.

Looking directly at the sun can cause permanent damage to the eye's retina.

Volcanoes produce a kind of natural glass called *obsidian*. It can be formed into a fine cutting edge that is sharper than a steel scalpel blade and is used in cardiac surgery.

The drug used to treat sleeping sickness contains arsenic and kills 10 percent of patients who receive it.

An exploding star is known as a *supernova* and produces as much energy in a few months as the sun would over billions of years.

There are 500,000 detectable earthquakes around the world each year.

Incandescent lightbulbs are extremely inefficient—95 percent of the power they use creates heat, so only 5 percent is used for the light itself.

First-century engineer Hero of Alexandria invented the first vending machine. It dispensed holy water!

British scientist Philip D'Arcy Hart lived until the age of 106 and was still doing research at the age of 100!

The *elasmosaurus* was a prehistoric marine reptile that weighed several metric tons. Its neck was so long that it made up over half its total length of 46 feet (14 meters).

The three main types of meteorite are made of stone, iron, or a mixture of the two.

If an ostrich really did bury its head in the sand, it would suffocate.

It may look fragile, but spider silk is very strong—tougher than steel wire of the same thickness!

Oil is made from the remains of plants and animals that lived millions of years ago. That's why it could eventually run out.

Peat moss can hold up to 20 times its dry weight in water, a bit like a sponge.

If you walked on the moon without a space suit you would get badly sunburned within a few seconds. Luckily, our planet's atmosphere keeps us from burning so quickly.

The people of Kathmandu in Nepal were shocked when it snowed in February 2007—it hadn't snowed there for 63 years!

The male mistle thrush senses when bad weather is coming and sings from the top of a tree or rooftop. It used to be known as a *storm cock*.

Oak trees don't produce acorns until they are 50 years old.

A *lungfish* can live out of water for up to 4 years! During dry seasons, it burrows into mud and breathes through a pair of basic lungs.

At least 90 percent of plants depend on fungi for their survival.

Dinosaurs roamed the earth for more than 100 million years.

A million meteors enter Earth's atmosphere every day! Luckily, most of them are only the size of a grain of sand.

Most people stay as far away as possible from a tornado, but American filmmaker Sean Casey wants to sit inside one. He has built the armor-plated Tornado Intercept Vehicle so that he can film a direct hit from a tornado and record its speed.

Potassium chloride is used to stop the heart during cardiac surgery.

Atoms are particles so tiny that 4 trillion would fit on this period.

New uniforms for the police in Gujarat, India, are impregnated with a permanent fresh flower and citrus fragrance. The latest fiber-optic technology means they can also be seen in the dark!

Light is the fastest thing in the universe and travels at around 300,000 kilometres (185,000 miles) per second.

Earmuffs were invented by a 15-year-old American boy in the 19th century!

Researchers have monitored the movements of bees by attaching tiny bar codes to them.

Some types of bamboo can grow 3 feet (90 centimeters) in a day. You can almost see them growing!

Tropical cloud forests are shrouded in mist most of the time. The lack of sunlight means that trees tend to be shorter than in rain forests and the ground is covered in moss.

In electronics, a jiffy is 1/60th of a second.

The *welwitschia* desert plant can live for more than a thousand years and looks like a stranded octopus! Its leaves separate into straggly strips that look like tentacles.

In parts of India, Brazil, and the US, car fuel is made from sugar!

Sand is mostly made from tiny pieces of the mineral *quartz*.

American engineer Percy Spencer invented the microwave oven after a chocolate bar melted in his pocket as he stood next to a radar tube.

The first traffic lights were manually operated red and green gaslights, placed outside London's Houses of Parliament. Unfortunately, they exploded and injured the policeman who was operating them.

The largest volcano is in Hawaii. It's more than 9 miles (15 kilometers) high, with its base in the sea.

It takes 1 day for Earth to rotate once on its axis. It doesn't last 24 hours but 23 hours, 56 minutes!

Siamese kittens are cream in color. As they grow, the coolest parts of the body darken, due to an enzyme in their hair that is heat-activated.

The daytime temperature on Mercury is about 806 degrees Fahrenheit (430 degrees Celsius). That's hot!

Drips of molten glass cooled in water form tadpole-shaped glass drops that shatter into a powder if the "tail" is tweaked. They are known as *Prince Rupert's drops* after their inventor, Prince Rupert of the Rhine, who used them to play jokes.

You can be struck by lightning even if you're indoors! A bolt can travel down phone lines, electric cables, and plumbing pipes, so keep away from them during an electrical storm.

When bacteria were first discovered, they were named *animalcules*.

Virga is rain that evaporates before it reaches the ground.

Water is 9 percent lighter when it's frozen—that's why your ice cubes float.

Baikal seals can be found only in Lake Baikal, Siberia. The lake is a long way from the ocean, so how they got there is a scientific mystery!

Sapphires can be brown, clear, gray, or black as well as blue.

The leaf of the giant Amazon water lily is so strong that you could sit on it without sinking!

It takes Saturn more than 29 years to orbit the sun.

Tyrannosaurus rex was so heavy that if it fell over, it would have died from the impact. Those little arms were no good for breaking its fall either!

The world's first hydroelectric power station used water from a lake to light a country house in Northumberland, England, in 1870.

Ultraviolet light from the sun has antiseptic properties. It causes sunburn, too!

Silver conducts heat and electricity more quickly than any other metal.

Mad Serbian scientist Nikola Tesla was obsessed with the number 3: he would have to walk around the block three times before entering a building and insisted that the number of any hotel room he stayed in be divisible by 3.

Young green tree pythons are yellow, red, or brown!

The ginkgo tree is a *living fossil*—that means it's a unique tree with no close living relatives and dates back 270 million years.

In 1930, a University of Queensland professor began an experiment with a funnel full of pitch (tar) to show his students how something that appears solid can be a liquid. The first drip took 10 years to fall, and the eighth drip fell in 2000. It will be a hundred years before all the pitch has dripped through, finishing the long, long experiment!

It rains at the same time every day in rain forests on the equator.

Some bacteria are sensitive to the earth's magnetic field. *Magnetotactic bacteria* all point to *magnetic north*.

Earthstars
**are mushrooms
that open up into a
star shape.**

Eighty percent of the world's
deserts aren't sandy but rocky.
Some are salt covered, and a
few are even icy.

You're electric! Your nervous
system is constantly sending
messages around the body by
electrical impulses.

A British scientist decided to take his four
children on a trek up part of Mount
Everest to research how their bodies
coped with low oxygen levels. That's
one way to earn your pocket
money, kids ...

The first raincoats designed by
Charles Macintosh were made
waterproof with rubber and
a by-product of coal tar. They kept people
dry, but the smell was horrible!

Raindrops aren't teardrop shaped: small ones are spherical, and larger ones are flat on the bottom—kind of hamburger-bun shaped!

The people of Siberia were surprised when they looked out one morning and saw a blanket of . . . orange snow! The reason for the freaky color remained a mystery, but it was believed to have been caused by pollution.

The World Wide Web was born in 1991. There are now over 1,000 million internet users globally!

Gold is the softest metal—a traditional test was to bite it and see if the teeth left a mark.

Finland has 187,888 lakes and 179,584 islands.

Diamonds are
so hard that only
other diamonds can
scratch them.

Until the 15th century, Christian
scholars believed that Jerusalem was
the center of the universe and that
Earth was a flat disk surrounded by
oceans.

The first alarm clocks were created
for monks in the 14th century to
make sure they didn't miss their
morning prayers!

Less than 1 percent of all the water on our planet is drinkable.

The planet Mars was named after the Roman
god of war because it looks red—the
color of blood.

It takes 10 minutes for rain to drip
through the dense leaves of a rain
forest and reach the forest floor.

The dodo bird was made extinct only 80 years after it was discovered.

American scientist Benjamin Franklin had bad eyesight and got so fed up with switching between different pairs of spectacles that he invented bifocals!

There's no such thing as bulletproof glass, only bullet-resistant glass. One-way bullet-resistant glass has recently been invented for armored vehicles, protecting the occupants but allowing them to defend themselves.

A third of the world's population is infected with tuberculosis (TB)—one person per second picks up the bacteria. Some people carry TB but do not become ill from it themselves.

Chalk is made from the fossilized skeletons of tiny sea animals!

The 10 highest mountains in the world are all in the Himalayas.

The Eiffel Tower is painted in three different colors! Because of the effects of light and background, three shades are needed to make it appear to be one color.

Some rocks can float! In a volcanic eruption, the violent separation of gas from lava produces a "frothy" rock called *pumice*, which is loaded with gas bubbles.

Flash floods and landslides unearthed an ancient tree trunk in Switzerland. The white pine trunk, believed to have been preserved in ice, was examined by experts and found to be 2,815 years old!

A hurricane north of the equator spins counter-clockwise, while a hurricane south of the equator will spin clockwise.

Yucca plants and yucca moths depend on each other for survival—the small moth is the only creature that can pollinate the plants as it feeds.

Every rainbow is unique: each rainbow is formed from light hitting your eye at a very precise angle. Someone standing next to you will see light coming from a slightly different angle than you and therefore see a different rainbow.

Pure water is a light shade of blue.

You can tell if an egg is hard boiled or not by spinning it: if the inside is solid, it will keep on spinning. If the egg is raw, the liquid contents will stop the egg's spinning within three rotations.

Even if it's not taken out of its packaging, a disposable battery will lose up to 25 percent of its power in a year.

There are earthquakes on the moon . . . called moonquakes, of course! There are also icequakes in Antarctica.

There are more than 150 giant craters around the world, left by fallen meteorites. The largest one is in Arizona—it measures more than 4,000 feet (1,200 meters) in diameter and was created about 50,000 years ago.

The cracks in breaking glass travel at more than 3,000 miles (5,000 kilometers) per hour.

Water can cut through steel! Water jet tools shoot water through a fine nozzle at such high pressure that the jet cuts metal—and it never needs sharpening.

German scientists Josef von Mering and Oskar Minkowski discovered diabetes when, out of curiosity, they removed the pancreas from a dog and monitored the effects.

Diamond dust is a kind of glittering polar fog made up of tiny ice crystals.

Nineteenth-century British chemist Humphry Davy was addicted to *nitrous oxide*—laughing gas!

Iron and sulfur compounds are present in eggs—if you hard-boil an egg for too long, those compounds will show up as a green coating around the yolk.

In the middle of the Atlantic, two of the rock plates that make up the surface of the earth—the African plate and the American plate—are moving apart at about the same speed as your fingernails grow.

Uranus was originally called the *Georgian Planet,* after King George III.

Salt and vinegar is an explosive combination! There is a spectacular chemical reaction when the two are mixed in large quantities. Don't try it yourself, though . . .

Earth is traveling through space at an astonishing 65,000 miles (108,000 kilometers) per hour!

Italian genius Leonardo da Vinci was a very busy man—in addition to being a painter and inventor, he was an engineer, anatomist, architect, astronomer, musician, scientist, sculptor, mathematician, and writer!

Burning potassium gives off a violet flame.

The largest, heaviest land animal that ever lived was *Argentinosaurus*. It grew to 115 feet (35 meters) long and weighed 80 to 100 metric tons.

There are a million bacteria in a milliliter of fresh water.

A total solar eclipse can be seen from the same place only once every 370 years.

Stainless steel and water can neutralize strong odors such as garlic and fish. Soap-shaped pieces of steel are available, but a spoon is just as effective!

The poison *arsenic* occurs naturally throughout the earth's crust and can pollute drinking water.

The moon used to be much closer to our planet than it is now! A billion years ago, it would take only 20 days to go around Earth, compared to the 27 days it takes now. It's still moving away by about 1.5 inches (4 centimeters) a year.

Despite being as big as several countries, China has only one time zone. Until 1949, it had five.

The biggest stars in the galaxy are called *supergiants* and *hypergiants*. A red *supergiant* can be 1,500 times bigger than the sun!

An oily plant substance called *petrichor* is what causes the refreshing smell after rainfall. Plants secrete it during dry periods and the scent is released when it rains.

Venus is shrouded in clouds of sulfur dioxide and sulfuric acid.

The hagfish secretes a unique slimy mucus—it's reinforced with fine, strong fibers similar to spider silk.

Long before Alexander Fleming discovered penicillin, ancient Egyptians and ancient Greeks recognized that some molds had antibacterial properties and used them for dressing wounds.

Migrating birds are sensitive to the earth's magnetic field and use it to guide them during their flights.

There were no polar ice caps 90 million years ago and Alaska was as warm as southern California is now!

Beer Crater on Mars is named after German astronomer Wilhelm Beer.

Baobab trees, also known as monkey bread trees, can store up to 120,000 liters (253,605 pints) of water in their trunks! This is to make sure they survive during long droughts.

Most colors have a wavelength, but brown doesn't. It's just a combination of other colors and their wavelengths.

CAUTION: Some of these World Record Facts involve dangerous activities. They have been set by people who have had proper medical guidance. Don't try any of them at home!

Sultan Hassanal Bolkiah of Brunei has the largest collection of Rolls-Royces: he owns about 150. He has 2,000 other luxury cars too!

Kilauea in Hawaii is the world's most active volcano and has been erupting non-stop since 1983.

American Ashrita Furman broke the fastest skipping record in 2007 by skipping 3.1 miles (5 kilometers) in 35 minutes, 19 seconds. He skipped at Tiger Temple in Thailand . . . and had a tiger trotting alongside him most of the way!

The youngest person to reach the top of Mount Everest was 15-year-old Ming Kipa Sherpa in 2003.

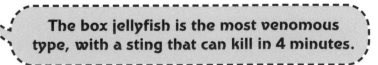

The box jellyfish is the most venomous type, with a sting that can kill in 4 minutes.

Joss Stone was the youngest BRIT Award winner when she won two awards at age 18 in 2005.

Astronomers spotted the fastest star in the galaxy in 2005. It was zooming through the Milky Way at more than 3.9 million kilometres (2.4 million miles) per hour!

The only known koala twins were born in 1999 in Queensland.

250,000 brightly colored power balls were used for the Sony Bravia TV advertisement—the most props ever used in a commercial.

The world's tallest building is Taipei 101 in Taiwan, which stands 1,666 feet (508 meters) high.

The bee hummingbird is the smallest bird: the male measures just 2.24 inches (57 millimeters) in length.

Russia has a record 15,000 circus performers.

The largest insectivore is the moon rat—a kind of hedgehog! Its full length is about 2 feet (60 centimeters).

The largest meteorite from Mars weighed 40 pounds (18 kilograms) and landed in Nigeria.

The longest cuddle ever lasted for 5,000 years! Archaeologists discovered a pair of entwined skeletons in northern Italy and believe the couple to be from the Neolithic period.

The world's smallest owl is the elf owl—it's the same size as a sparrow!

A record number of 269 Asian elephants gathered to eat over 11,231 pounds (50 metric tons) of fruit and vegetables at Thailand's 2003 annual elephant parade.

Some places on the earth are covered in salt! The largest salt flats are in Bolivia, where 10 billion metric tons of salt cover an area of 4,600 square miles (12,000 square kilometers).

The youngest FIFA World Cup Final scorer is Pelé, who was just 17 when he scored for Brazil in 1958.

How many Australians can you get on a surfboard? Forty-seven on a specially designed one, and they all rode a wave on it!

The US has the largest air force in the world, with more than 6,000 aircraft.

The smallest spy plane isn't much bigger than your hand! The *Black Widow* was developed to carry a miniature video camera.

The longest-ever backwards motorcycle journey was completed by a group of 14 members of the Swedish Army Lions motorcycle display team. They rode their Husaberg 400 cc bikes backward for a distance of 10.87 miles (17.5 kilometers) to commemorate the 600th anniversary of their hometown, Skövde.

The world's biggest aquarium opened in 2005 in Atlanta. The Georgia Aquarium contains more than 100,000 sea creatures.

Creme Puff the cat lived to the ripe old age of 38 years, 3 days! That's nearly 350 cat years!

At the age of 22, Fernando Alonso became the youngest driver to win a Formula 1 World Championship race when he won the 2003 Hungarian Grand Prix.

The oldest person to grow a new tooth was 61.

Thieves staged the largest-ever jewel robbery when they got away with $100 million worth of gems from the Antwerp World Diamond Center in 2003.

Hurricane Wilma was the strongest hurricane ever, with wind speeds reaching 165 miles (270 kilometers) per hour.

The longest word in the English language is the name of a lung disease called *pneumonoultramicroscopicsilicovolcanoconiosis.*

Dr. Who is the longest-running science-fiction TV series. The BBC broadcast the first episode in 1963.

The fastest tennis serve came from American Andy Roddick and was measured at 153 miles (246.2 kilometers) per hour.

Three children in the Norwegian Henriksen family were born 4 years apart on a leap day (February 29).

American Richard Presley lived in an underwater module for 69 days, 19 minutes, as part of research into the effects of living under the sea.

Northern Irish men have the highest rate of heart disease in the world.

Daredevil Stephen Brown rode a motorcycle through a tunnel of fire that was 167 feet (51 meters) long.

American cyclist Scott Koons cycled 13.15 miles (21.16 kilometers) around a track with no hands. Hasn't anyone told him that's dangerous?

North and South America make up the largest area of land named after one person—15th-century Italian explorer Amerigo Vespucci.

Addwaitya the giant tortoise was the world's oldest animal! He died in India at the grand old age of 255 and his 5-foot (1.5-meter)-wide shell later went on display at a local museum.

The biggest recorded meteor shower fell over the Pacific Ocean in 1966, when 40,000 shooting stars shot across the sky in 20 minutes.

The gecko is the only lizard that makes noises.

German Johann Traber performed the fastest motorcycle wheelie on a tightrope in 2005 by traveling at 32 miles (53 kilometers) per hour!

Steve Griffiths and Philip John have both been bog-snorkeling world champions three times.

The world's longest banana split was more than 4 miles (7 kilometers) long!

Russian cosmonaut Valeriy Polyakov holds the record for the longest spaceflight in history—he spent 437 days in space and orbited Earth more than 7,000 times!

The most brightly colored dolphin is the Chinese pink dolphin. Its color comes from the large number of blood vessels near the surface of its skin.

The world's first female prime minister was Sri Lankan Sirimavo Bandaranaike, who took office in 1960.

Surinam in South America has the fewest movie theaters per population—one movie theater for more than 436,000 people!

A watermelon is 92 percent water—the highest percentage of any fruit.

Speed skater Jiajun Li from China took just 1 minute, 24 seconds, to get around a 3280 foot (1000-meter) track in 2004.

The *bunchberry dogwood* flower opens its petals in 0.5 millisecond!

The shark's sense of smell is greater than that of any other fish—it can detect one part of blood in 100 million parts of water.

The wettest place on earth is the Indian town of Cherrapunji, with an average annual rainfall of 38 feet, 2 inches (11.43 meters).

More than 200 million people have visited the Eiffel Tower since it was built, making it the world's most visited monument.

A record 6,272 pounds (2,844 kilograms) of plasticine was used to make Aardman Animation's *Wallace and Gromit: The Curse of the Were-Rabbit.*

The largest pink lake is in Senegal and measures 1 by 3 miles (1.5 by 5 kilometers). Its color comes from minerals and microorganisms.

Spiders Arabella and Anita were the first to spin webs in space in 1973!

The US produces more household waste per person than any other nation.

Sir Don Bradman (Australia) and Brian Lara (Trinidad and Tobago) are the only two batsmen in Test match cricket to have scored two innings of more than 300 runs.

The *howler monkey* is the loudest land animal—its call can be heard more than 3 miles (5 kilometers) away. The red howler monkey is the noisiest!

The fastest carrot chopper in the West is British TV chef James Martin—he peeled and chopped 18 ounces (515 grams) in 1 minute!

The worst air show disaster happened in 2002, when a fighter jet crashed into spectators in Ukraine and killed 78 people, injuring more than 100.

French skater Stephane Alfano performed a record 16 consecutive flat spins on inline skates in 2005.

The Jamaican iguana is the rarest lizard: only about 100 exist.

The largest living structure on earth is the Great Barrier Reef in Australia—it's over 1,200 miles (2,000 kilometers) long!

The heaviest object ever weighed was the launchpad Revolving Service Structure (RSS) at NASA's Kennedy Space Center in Florida. The RSS weighed 5,342,000 pounds (2,423 metric tons).

The longest TV advertisement was for Lipton Green Iced Tea and lasted a snoozy 24 minutes.

The youngest person to reach the South Pole was 18-year-old Sarah Ann McNair-Landry in 2005.

German golfers Eric Kirchner and Patrick Herresthal played 6 rounds of golf in 6 different countries in 1 day!

Adám Lörincz was the world's youngest musical composer at 14 years, 76 days, when his musical, *Star of the King*, was performed on August 16, 2002, in Hungary.

American Mike "Rooftop" Escamilla holds the record for the longest BMX backflip at a distance of 62 feet, 2 inches (18.94 meters).

Top Dubai chefs made a date and banana cake that stretched along the seafront for 8,303 feet (2,530 meters) in 1996.

The *Arctic tern* has the longest migration of any bird—it breeds in the Arctic, flies south to Antarctica during the northern winter, then flies back again!

Russia has 11 time zones, more than any other country.

Chelsea soccer club player Frank Lampard played in a record 160 consecutive Premiership matches.

The world's largest ice hotel is in Sweden and is built every year in December.

The fastest production car is the Bugatti Veyron, which can be driven at speeds of more than 248 miles (400 kilometers) per hour.

The largest ocean is the Pacific—it makes up 45.9 percent of the world's oceans.

The world's most premature surviving baby was Amillia Taylor, who was just the length of a ballpoint pen when she was born at less than 22 weeks.

German race car driver Michael Schumacher holds two world records: he has won the most Grand Prix races (83) and the most World Championships in Formula 1 (7).

The longest earthquake lasted for 10 minutes in the Sumatra-Andaman islands.

A US restaurant produced the world's biggest burger for a charity event. It contained an 80-pound (48-kilogram) beef patty and 160 cheese slices!

Enormous hailstones caused around $1 billion worth of damage during a 1984 storm in Munich, Germany, making it the worst damage toll from a hailstorm.

The highest internet café in the world is at Mount Everest base camp, more than 16,600 feet (5,000 meters) above sea level.

American Timothy Turner Hayes had skied on every continent except Antarctica by the age of 14.

The smallest animal trained to detect land mines is the honeybee!

Scottish store owner Selim Sener set a world record when he wrapped 10 portions of fries in 1 minute for a National Chip Week event.

Athletes Justin Gatlin (US) and Asafa Powell (Jamaica) have both run the 100-meter race in 9.77 seconds. See how quickly you can do it!

Dallas golden retriever Augie could hold five tennis balls in his mouth at once!

The world's leading ice cream eaters are the Australians, gobbling 3.6 gallons (16.6 liters) per person each year.

The largest hoard of coins was discovered in 1908, when 150,000 13th-century coins were unearthed in Belgium.

The noisiest spider is the European buzzing spider. The male makes a buzzing sound as it vibrates its abdomen against a leaf to attract a mate.

Jupiter is the largest planet in the solar system: it's more than 300 times bigger than Earth!

American rapper 50 Cent had a record three singles in the US Billboard Top Ten in 2005: *Candy Shop, How We Do* and *Disco Inferno.*

The largest toothpick sculpture was Alligator Alley, made by American Michael Smith from more than 3 million toothpicks!

The puma is known by 40 different names, the most for any animal.

Karen Davies of Britain has won the toe-wrestling world championships a record four times.

The fastest lava flow burst from Nyiragongo in the Democratic Republic of Congo at 40 miles (60 kilometers) per hour.

In 2005,
Hans Van Dan
Helzen from the US
completed 51 yo-yo
tricks in 1
minute!

Japan's *Big O* is the world's first centerless Ferris wheel. It has Tokyo's biggest roller coaster running right through it.

The highest temperature recorded in the shade was 136 degrees Fahrenheit (58 degrees Celsius) at Al-Aziziyah in Libya. That was in 1922, before anyone had even heard of global warming!

Astronaut Helen Sharman was the first Briton in space in 1991.

American Dale Webster surfed every day between September 2, 1975, and February 29, 2004, chalking-up a record 10,407 consecutive days of surfing. Awesome!

Brazilian soccer star Ronaldo has scored 15 World Cup Final goals.

The *sailfish* can whiz along at a record speed of 60 miles (100 kilometers) per hour.

American Ron Scarpa has been barefoot waterskiing world champion four times. Waterskiing barefoot is an achievement in itself!

Canada's Rideau Canal Skateway is 4.8 miles (7.8 kilometers) long and is the largest naturally frozen ice rink.

Australian Kay Cottee was the first woman to sail around the world solo and nonstop in 1988.

The dumbo octopus, so called because of its flapping frills that look like an elephant's ears, lives deeper in the ocean than any other octopus at 5,000 feet (1,500 meters).

A budgerigar named Puck knew a record 1,728 words before he died in 1994.

The lowest temperature endured by a bird is minus 4 degrees Fahrenheit (minus 20 degrees Celsius), the Antarctic chill felt by emperor penguins.

American Gary Duschl has been collecting gum wrappers for more than 40 years. He has linked more than a million wrappers to make a record-breaking chain that is more than 45,000 feet (14,000 meters) long!

American Milburn Hart did a parachute jump at the age of 96 years, 63 days. It's never too late!

Wacky scientist Nikola Tesla created the longest man-made bolt of lightning in his lab in 1899. It was 130 feet (40 meters) long and could be heard for miles.

The longest wall is the Great Wall of China. At 2,150 miles (3,460 kilometers), it's three times the length of Britain.

Kathryn Ratcliffe ate 170 Smarties in 3 minutes . . . using chopsticks. You can try that one at home!

The carnivorous plants that devour the largest prey are from the *Nepenthacae* family. The Asian rain forest plants can digest frogs, birds, and rats.

The largest kangaroo is as tall as a man! The red kangaroo can be up to 5 feet, 11 inches (1.8 meters) tall.

The smallest nest is built by the vervain hummingbird and is the size of half a walnut shell!

The most heat-tolerant organism lives in the boiling-hot hydrothermal vents at the bottom of the Pacific Ocean. Bacteria-like *strain 121* can survive temperatures of 250 degrees Fahrenheit (121 degrees Celsius).

Ashrita Furman of the US jumped 23.11 miles (37.18 kilometers) on a pogo stick in 1997.

Uruguan Emilio Arenas Florin began collecting key rings in 1955 and now has more than 25,630!

In 2003, American Jay Stokes made 534 parachute jumps in 24 hours. That's a jump every 2.5 minutes, and a lot of them were in the rain!

The oldest playable instrument is a 9,000-year-old Chinese flute, made from a bird's leg bone.

The fastest FIFA World Cup red card issued went to Uruguayan player José Batista, 56 seconds into the 1986 match against Scotland.

Pharaoh Phiops II ruled for a record 94 years from the age of 6.

Australian Kareena Oates set the hula hoop world record in 2005, with 100 hoops at once. See how many you can manage!

The world's longest hot dog was 57 feet, 4 inches (17.5 meters) long!

The oldest commissioned warship still afloat is the USS Constitution, which has been part of the US Navy since 1797.

The Japanese are the biggest comics readers. Their *manga* comics account for 40 percent of all printed material sold.

The African *patas* monkey can race along the ground at 34 miles (55 kilometers) an hour, making it the fastest primate.

The highest number of international goals scored by a female soccer player is 144, by American Mia Hamm.

The deepest half marathon took place in a Polish salt mine at a depth of 695 feet (212 meters).

US astronauts Eugene Cernan and Harrison Schmitt took the longest moonwalk in 1972. They spent more than 7 hours outside their module and explored 12.6 miles (20.4 kilometers) of the moon's surface.

The largest number of living creatures produced during a magic performance was 80,000 bees in a Penn and Teller show.

The largest set of Russian nesting dolls (*matrioshkas*) contained 51 pieces that were hand-painted by artist Youlia Bereznitskaya. The smallest doll was just 0.12 inches (3 millimeters) high!

The first Olympic Games was held in 776 BC.

The largest same-name gathering took place in 2005, when 1,096 Mohammeds got together in Dubai.

Peter Jackson's third *Lord of the Rings* film, *The Return of the King*, won a record 11 Oscars.

The *peacock mantis* shrimp has the strongest animal punch! Its front leg moves at 75 feet (23 meters) per second to club its prey.

Louisiana's second bridge of the Lake Pontchartrain Causeway is the world's longest bridge at 23.8 miles (38.4 kilometers) long. If you stand in the middle of it, you can't see either end!

Australian Minnie Munro became the oldest bride when she got married at the age of 102.

The youngest person to visit the wreck of the *Titanic* was 13-year-old Sebastian Harris in 2005.

The American *Achaearenea tepidariorium* spider has the strongest known web, tough enough to ensnare a mouse.

Mandarin Chinese is the most popular spoken language in the world, with 915 million speakers.

Nineteen scuba divers took part in the largest underwater cycle race in Guernsey, UK, in 2005.

Elvis Presley is the richest dead celebrity. He earned $45 million in 2005 alone.

Britons lead the world in baked bean consumption! They eat 11 pounds, 10 ounces (5.3 kilograms) per person per year—about four times more than people in the US!

As part of his job, American W. R. "Rusty" Haight was a human crash-test dummy in a record 718 collisions.

The longest nonstop commercial airline flight was from Hong Kong to London and took 22 hours, 42 minutes.

Unbelievable
Random Facts

The Empire State Building is struck by lightning about 100 times every year.

A nearsighted Croatian granddad sparked a police manhunt when he went to collect his grandson from day care and took the wrong boy home!

World War II veteran Don Karkos had been blind for 64 years after receiving a shrapnel wound. His sight was miraculously restored when he was head-butted by the racehorse he was looking after!

There are no donkeys in the Donkey Kong computer game.

Carhenge on the Nebraska plains is a replica of England's Stonehenge . . . made with 38 vintage cars that are painted gray!

There are more than 32,000 radio stations around the world.

Fake snow used to be made from asbestos, so people would have sprinkled the toxic mineral around their homes!

A Swiss pilot designed wings and jet engines that could be strapped to his back and allow him to fly. He couldn't run fast enough to take off, though—he had to jump from an airborne airplane!

Hawaiians consume more Spam than anyone else in the world.

Cop is short for constable on patrol.

Watermelon snow is found in California's Sierra Nevada. Algae make it pink, and it smells of watermelon too!

Some twins create their own language, known as *cryptophasia*, that only they can understand.

A sick Yorkshire terrier was found by a vet to have swallowed eight party balloons. After they were removed, it must have felt a little deflated!

Bao Xishun, the world's tallest man, saved the lives of two dolphins in 2006 by reaching into their stomachs with his long arms, which measure 42 inches (1.06 meters), and removing pieces of plastic.

Blue *snow fleas* can be spotted hopping around on the snow on a winter's day.

Attempting to go over Niagara Falls is illegal. Several people have been drowned or injured doing so.

A crazy Romanian man named his baby daughter after one of his favorite Mercedes cars: SLK. If he'd had a boy, he would have named him BMW!

Japanese kimono makers don't just throw away their broken needles; they hold a special festival for them! During *harikuyo*, the women thank the needles for their hard work and place them in a slab of tofu.

A dog had to be rescued by coast guards after it ran off the edge of a cliff while chasing seagulls.

A British survey of 2,000 people showed that more men than women take a cuddly toy to bed with them.

Stewardesses is the longest word that can be typed using just the left-hand part of a computer keyboard.

Australian banknotes are waterproof.

Red rain fell in the Indian state of Kerala in 2001. The reason for the strange color is still a mystery, but theories range from algae spores or pollution to the blood of bats or extraterrestrials!

The Japanese believe that a clean toilet brings good fortune. They even have books on the subject!

More than 25 percent of the world's natural gas reserves are in Russia.

The Eiffel Tower sways up to 3 inches (nearly 7 centimeters) in the wind.

A great-grandmother outdid her fishing champion husband on a family vacation in Florida by catching a shark 9 feet (2.7 meters) long!

Al Capone's business card said he was a used furniture dealer.

Australia has a plague of poisonous cane toads, which can grow to be the size of a small dog. The government has asked people to kill them humanely, but most Australians just bash them over the head!

The name for the Volkswagen Beetle in Bulgarian translates as *Volkswagen Turtle*.

A Japanese man was so angry at a new building blocking out his light that he shot it, causing lots of damage and getting himself arrested!

The US Mint discovered that the words *In God We Trust* were missing from some of their $1 coins in 2007. Since coins with faults are valuable to collectors, one was sold on eBay for $405!

A fighter jet and a surface-to-air missile were put up for sale on a Chinese auction website. You really can buy anything on the internet!

The average person spends 2 years of his or her life on the telephone.

Helium is made up of lightweight atoms which can escape easily—that's why your balloons go down so quickly!

188 million Valentine's cards are exchanged every year.

Voice actor Mel Blanc was known as *the man of a thousand voices*, but he denied this—he said he had provided only 850! His most famous characters were Bugs Bunny and Daffy Duck.

Advertising that targets children under the age of 12 is banned in Sweden.

Many types of trees benefit from forest fires, and some need them to regenerate.

A Bosnian man faked his own death to see who would attend his funeral. Only his mother showed up!

A Serbian soccer player who was dropped from his club got even by churning up the pitch with a tractor.

150 saffron crocuses are needed to produce 0.04 ounce (1 gram) of the spice saffron.

Satellite navigation systems can't always be trusted. Drivers following instructions have ended up in the river in a little village in Wiltshire, England, and now locals are charging $49 to pull them out!

The word for *taxi* is the same in 13 languages.

A Nebraska man saved his dog with mouth-to-mouth resuscitation after it fell into an icy lake while chasing geese.

It took 14 years to build the Sydney Opera House.

The population of the world is 6.6 billion—more than 203,000 babies are born every day!

The largest charity donation in American history is $30 billion, given by businessman and philanthropist Warren Buffet to the Bill and Melinda Gates Foundation.

The Sargasso Sea has no coastline—it's in the middle of the North Atlantic Ocean.

Johnny Herbert came fifth in the 1989 US Grand Prix, but a local American firm refused to rent him a car because he was under 25.

Only three cricketers have ever scored the maximum of 36 runs in an over (bowling six consecutive balls in succession)—Garfield Sobers in 1968, Ravi Shastri in 1985, and Herschelle Gibbs in 2007.

The first item ever to have its bar code scanned was a pack of chewing gum.

As Jonny Wilkinson scored the goal that sent the England rugby team to World Cup victory in 2003, his mother was out shopping at her local supermarket!

It's illegal to keep a gerbil as a pet in California, since gerbils sometimes carry tuberculosis.

A Chinese couple were in such a rush to meet relatives that they left their 3-year-old son behind on the plane!

You took your life in your hands playing soccer in its formative years. In the 1905 season, 18 players were killed and 150 seriously injured.

50,000 text messages are sent every minute around the world.

Japan has the highest number of vending machines: one for every 23 people. They sell anything from live lobsters to potted plants!

College lecturer Paul Rogerson creates award-winning sculptures . . . from lard! His works of characters from Bugs Bunny to Don Quijote last only 2 months before they spoil and become stinky.

Snap, crackle, pop in German is knisper, knasper, knusper!

There are around 1,250 Boeing 737s in the air around the world at any one time.

A Mexican mail-man was arrested after police officers found 22,400 pounds (10 metric tons) of undelivered letters at his house.

The Chicago River is dyed green every year to celebrate St. Patrick's Day.

A beauty contest for retirees has been launched in Switzerland ... called Miss Retirement Home! Plans are now under way for a Mr. Retirement Home competition.

An elderly woman who died in the economy section of an airplane shortly after takeoff was moved to first class for the remainder of the long flight. The things people will do to get an upgrade ...

Pablo Picasso, Leonardo da Vinci, and Paul McCartney all have roses named after them.

Saw-scaled vipers make a sizzling sound.

More than 700 languages are spoken in Indonesia.

An American who had his glasses broken and eye bruised by a snowball decided to sue the thrower for more than $3,800. Snow joke!

Parachutes have a hole in the top! The modern design lets built-up air through, which in old parachutes used to cause a swinging motion.

It's offensive to call an Inuit person an Eskimo.

Police in Soweto, South Africa, were called out to deal with attacks on pedestrians ... by giant rats! The scary rodents were nesting in old cars and protested if people passed by.

The prehistoric *Protosphyraena* was a bit like a swordfish but with the advantage of razor-sharp serrated front fins, with which it would slice the flesh of its prey.

A Cologne couple were locked inside a movie theater for the night after they fell asleep during a movie.

There are three golf balls on the moon.

The first ATM was installed in a New York bank in 1939 but taken out 6 months later because customers didn't like it. There were no more for 25 years after that!

A British man blinded in an accident had his sight restored 9 years later when he was struck by lightning.

There were no vehicles on Pitcairn Island in the South Pacific until the early 1970s.

The Palanga Amber Museum in Lithuania has a collection of about 28,000 pieces of amber, half of which contain fossilized insects, spiders, or plants.

In the US, more than 150 pairs of identical twins are married to identical twins!

Bookkeeper is the only word in the English language with three sets of double letters together.

Ice hockey was invented in Montreal, Canada, in 1875.

A day (sunrise to sunrise) on the planet Mercury is longer than its year (one orbit around the sun).

Buddhist monks refused to kill any of the ants infesting their temple in Kuala Lumpur, Malaysia, because of their beliefs in non-violence . . . even when one monk was hospitalized by ant bites!

Of the 40 horses that began the 2001 Grand National horse race in England, only two finished without stopping.

Bulgarian American singer Bantcho Bantchevsky is most famous for killing himself during the interval of an opera by jumping off a balcony at the Metropolitan Opera in New York.

Beards are banned by the US Army and Marine Corps.

Indian yellow paint pigment was originally made from the dried urine of cows that had been fed on only mango leaves and water.

A man was banned from a pub in Scotland . . . because he kept doing smelly farts!

If you multiply 21,978 by 4, the number you get is its mirror image—87,912. Try it and see!

An Israeli plane was delayed when a little bird flew into the cockpit as passengers were boarding. The passengers had to leave the plane and wait several hours while a professional bird catcher was called to remove it.

The first cup of coffee drunk on the moon was in 1969.

A middle-aged Chinese bachelor placed an advertisement asking for someone to share his grave—so he wouldn't be lonely in the afterlife!

Some sniffer dogs can track down pirate CDs and DVDs—they're trained to detect the chemicals used to make them.

A golf ball has about 400 dimples on it. The dimples make the ball travel farther.

Real gold and silver are sometimes used to decorate candy and desserts! One New York restaurant lists *Golden Opulence* on its menu, an ice cream sundae covered in 23-carat edible gold leaf.

The Pentagon is the world's biggest office building and has six zip codes all to itself.

Velcro comes from the French words for velvet (*velours*) and hook (*crochet*). Its inventor got the idea from sticky burrs on his clothes after a walk!

Ancient Egyptians loved cats and would shave off their eyebrows to mourn the death of one.

And finally...your bonus half fact. Can you complete it yourself?

An orangutan named Fu Manchu repeatedly escaped from his cage in an American zoo by...

Farting on the lock